Cat
Be Good

Cat
Be Good

A Foolproof Guide for the Complete
Care and Training of Your Cat

Annie Bruce

Adams Media
Avon, Massachusetts

Published by
Adams Media, an F+W Publications Company
57 Littlefield Street, Avon, MA 02322. U.S.A.
www.adamsmedia.com

ISBN: 1-59337-411-9

Printed in Canada.

J I H G F E D C B A

Library of Congress Cataloging-in-Publication Data
Bruce, Annie.
Cat be good : a foolproof guide for the complete care and training of your cat / by Annie Bruce.
p.   cm.
Originally published: Boulder, CO : Good Cats Wear Black, ©2000.
Includes bibliographical references.
ISBN 1-59337-411-9
1. Cats—Training. 2. Cats—Behavior. I. Title.
SF446.6.B78 2005
636.8—dc22
2005017393

This book is available at quantity discounts for bulk purchases.
For information, please call 1-800-872-5627.

This book is dedicated—

To those who have been
sick,
abused,
abandoned,
forgotten.

In memory of my wonderful mother and father,
Ruth and Emillano Coloma.

To Bruce, Sherri, Constance, Catalina,
David, Emillia, and Sarah Jane.

And in special memory of Moses.
May the slavery end.

Love,
Annie Bruce

Contents

ix   Foreword
xi   Acknowledgments

1   Part 1. Cat Basics
3   Introduction
5   1 ● The Truth About Cats
10   2 ● Safety
17   3 ● Adoption
29   4 ● The Newcomer
34   5 ● Fix 'em Good!
37   6 ● Change Happens
46   7 ● Litter Boxes Etc.
56   8 ● Lost and Found
61   9 ● Neighbors
67   10 ● Cat Beds

71   Part 2. Cat Life
73   11 ● Scratching Posts, Exercise, and Play
86   12 ● Diet
100   13 ● Hands-On Experience
104   14 ● Hair and Nails
111   15 ● Doctor, Doctor!
117   16 ● Administering Treatments
121   17 ● Yucky Stuff

sidebar key

true story

did you know?

helpful hints

warning!

general info

127   **Part 3. Cat Behavior**
129   18 ● Basic Training
138   19 ● Outside/Inside
153   20 ● Aggression
162   21 ● Litter Box Blues
179   22 ● Miscellaneous Problems

191   **Part 4. Aging**
193   23 ● Growing Old and Saying Goodbye

199   **Appendix**
201   Declawing Drawbacks
214   Cute Cat Tricks
217   Cat Maintenance Schedule
220   Cat Advocacy
228   Donations Needed
231   Products and Resources

247   Index

252   Poem
254   About the Author

255   Condensed Version of *Cat Be Good*
256   Important Facts About Declawed Cats

Foreword

by Dr. Nicholas Dodman

Annie Bruce is a dyed-in-the-wool cats' rights advocate and aficionado—good for her, good for cats, and good for you if you want to share in her insights by reading her book. Annie lives for cats and champions their cause. If you were a cat you would want Annie on your side to campaign against the travesties that may beset you. Annie has carefully considered how cats like to live, what they like to eat, what bothers them, and what causes them to act out what we perceive as their misbehaviors.

In this book she shares her wisdom—painstakingly assembled over years and carefully organized and illustrated for the reader's convenience. An index directs the reader to topics like hairballs, catnip, urine spraying, furniture scratching, and so on. You can learn why hairballs occur, how to recognize them, and how to minimize their occurrence; what catnip does to cats and why; the motivation for and environmental treatment for urine spraying; how to understand and redirect furniture scratching; and so much more (Annie firmly opposes declawing, as I do).

This book also contains information about where to go to get additional information on products and resources, how to contact cat advocacy groups, how to donate to cat charities, etc. There are cat vignettes, quotations about cats, even a poem Annie authored thrown in for good measure. The book is basically everything a 100 percent cat person could possibly write down to help other cat owners do the best for their cats and thus prevent stresses that cause problems for both cats and their owners.

Annie has pulled no punches, spared no amount of research, and told it as she sees it for the benefit of cat owners—and, more important, for their four-footed feline friends. Anecdotal and empirical, mythical and factual, fun-filled and serious, this book deals with all common cat issues as a text or reference. Read and enjoy.

Nicholas Dodman BVMS, MRCVS, DACVB
Professor and Behaviorist, Tufts University
Author: *The Cat Who Cried for Help* and *If Only They Could Speak*

Acknowledgments

This book would not have been possible without the talent, assistance, and dedication of many wonderful people. I am very grateful for their help, support, and patience.

Neil Feineman contributed greatly to this book and to my sanity. Neil graciously stepped in to help after I ran out of hope and resources. He got Josh, Pam, David, and James on board. And he helped write, edit, and organize this project to completion. His patience, persistence, and dedication were extraordinary. Neil's allergy to cats makes him all that more dedicated to getting the job done.

Josh Gunn deserves special recognition. He turned a draft into a manuscript. His rewriting changed the book from an unyielding conglomeration of data into a coherent collection of sensibly organized chapters.

More than anyone, my husband, Bruce Delaplain, knows how to get down to what I meant to say. His meticulous questions, reviews, and editing were critical to this book. Bruce cooked dinners and washed dishes while I wrote about cats, and he invented the title *Cat Be Good*. Bruce loves cats almost as much as I do. He is a great chef and I'd be lost without him.

Thanks to Stephanie Roth-Nelson for her scheduling, publishing efforts, and enthusiasm. Her editing and organization of the initial draft were important building blocks in the book's production.

Special gratitude goes to Diane Dietrich. Diane taught me about pet food and the role that diet plays in a cat's health and behavior. Diane played an important part in helping me develop these commonsense techniques for cat behavior. She has helped thousands of animals through proper diet.

My friend Harriet Baker is a very special lady. Harriet's strength, persistence, and dedication to ending declawing is inspiring. I believe that Harriet has done more to help cats than any person I have ever met.

Pam Ferdinand provided her remarkable copyediting skills and her intellect. Pam got the text consistent and taught me more about writing.

An extra-special thanks to David Levine, who designed the first edition of this book (logo, style, and cover). I really appreciate his advice. Thanks also to Steve "Crusher" Bartlett, who helped with the styling and production of that book.

Many have helped review portions of this book. Their input was invaluable. I'd like to thank Edward John Mills, H.C. Leeds, Constance Krupka, Esther Mechler of SPAY/USA, Anupam Barlow, Kathleen Geary, Celia Bennett, Jerrilyn Rooney, Barbara Perin, Joy Matey-Yetman, and Dr. J. Douglas Courtley, DVM.

The friendship and support of dancers also helped make this book possible. Thank you Motion Underground Dance Company, Kenny Jimenez, Vital Signs, Teri Kutsko, LuAnn Sessions, Meriku Lewis, Sarah J. Salsich, Penny Peterson, Sandy Sherman, Marcus Hilgers, Omar Bose, Chris Moore, David A. Alexander, Troy Burrell, Ying-Fon Chang, and each and every dancer at Motion Underground. Motion Underground is a nonprofit dance company/"community." This book would not have been possible without the fun, exercise, and encouragement I have received at Motion Underground. MU helps keep kids off the streets by providing a supportive and enjoyable dance/learning environment. Diligent efforts of volunteers and teachers are under the direction of owner, world-class instructor, and choreographer Ken Jimenez (*www.MotionUnderground.com*).

A special thanks needs to be given to the rest of my friends and support group: Sherri Brando, Ken Mineni, Aunt Irma James, Kathleen Hansen, Yolanda Hagan, Gary Lowenthal, Catalina Hall, Stanley Mitchell, Megan Mitchell, Louis Krupka, David and LaVon Sonne, Shana Wagner, Jill Harrison, Francesca Militeau, Karen Lerner, Jay Leber, Jill Jones, Reverend Jack Groverland, and Mr. Jones.

A very big thank-you to these caring and courageous pet professionals, whose efforts improve the lives of cats: Harriet Baker of The Cat Catalyst; Rene Knapp of Helping Paws; Dr. Jennifer Conrad, DVM, of The Paw Project; Dr. Nicholas Dodman, professor and behaviorist, Tufts University; Dr. Aubrey Lavizzo, DVM, of Plaza Veterinary Clinic; Dr. Gloria Binkowski, DVM, of The Vet at the Barn; Dr. Kimberly Harrison, DVM; Jackson Galaxy and Dr. Jean Hofve, DVM, of Little Big Cat; Hal and Judy Abrams of Animal Radio; Willow Evans; Marge Satterfield; Susan Easterly; Beth Springer of Good Samaritan Pet Center; Lisa and Sam Booker of Every Creature Counts; and Karen Gnaegy of Animal Rescue and Adoption Society.

And a very, very special thanks to all the cat owners who have come to me for help. With each question you have taught me a little bit more about cats.

I apologize if I missed anyone. I didn't mean to.

Part 1
Cat Basics

3		Introduction
5	1 ●	The Truth About Cats
10	2 ●	Safety
17	3 ●	Adoption
29	4 ●	The Newcomer
34	5 ●	Fix 'em Good!
37	6 ●	Change Happens
46	7 ●	Litter Boxes Etc.
56	8 ●	Lost and Found
61	9 ●	Neighbors
67	10 ●	Cat Beds

Introduction

🐾 The day my cat Simon attacked me was the day I really started learning about cats. It was a hot August day in Detroit. I was 15 years old and playing rough with my cat. He wasn't neutered; back then, most male cats weren't. And I made the mistake of thinking my three-year-old cat would never—*could* never—hurt me.

Simon was becoming agitated from my rough handling of him. I ignored the swish of his tail, his hunched back, and his heavy breathing, and continued to wrestle with him. After I quit and walked away, I turned around and saw Simon's angry glare. He leapt and flew across the room at me, tore into my right arm with all fours, and sank his teeth deep into my bicep. The violence left me stunned and terribly injured. I couldn't use my arm for more than a month. That's what just *one* bite from a cat can do.

I'd had cats for six years by then, and hadn't even started to realize their potential.

For a few days, I thought about getting rid of Simon, but because I had provoked him that hardly seemed fair. Eventually I worked through my fear, Simon remained a good friend, and he never hurt me again.

Ever since that time, I've been learning about cats, frequently through mistakes. I have found things that work and things that don't. I've learned how to have cats that don't tear up our fine carpet and furniture and listen to what I tell them—without my having to do much work or spend much money. I'd rather spend money on fun stuff or cat toys than on cat doctors or home repairs.

Now, after owning and learning about cats for almost fifty years, I find myself a cat behaviorist. Actually, I call myself a "cat owner consultant" because I am expert at being a cat owner now, and my primary goal is to help other *owners*. There are a lot of outdated beliefs, bad advice, and convincing advertising for bad products out there. Using a squirt bottle is just one example. And it's both the cat and the owner who will pay, sometimes dearly, for being misinformed.

I wrote *Cat Be Good* so that you will not only have cats but that you'll have *good* cats, for a very long time. Cats aren't really mysterious, though we have been led to believe they are. You'll find out that cats do listen, they will learn, and that your cat really can be good.

Let's get started!

1 The Truth About Cats

Cats have acquired an undeserved reputation for being untrainable, but nothing could be further from the truth. Cats are smart. They listen. And they are trainable.

Many people assume that cats are antisocial and unattached. They think nothing of leaving a cat alone for long periods of time. These things are not true. Cats shouldn't be left alone any more than people, dogs, or birds should. Cats *hunt* alone, but they prefer company the rest of the time.

A Parade of Myths

These are just a few of the other myths that have caused misfortune to many cats. Many of these myths have begun only in the last few decades.

- Cats always land on their feet.
- Indoor cats must be declawed.
- Declawing saves time and money.
- Cats do not like to have their paws touched.
- Spanking a cat is effective punishment.
- Diet and exercise aren't important to cats.
- Black cats are bad luck.

Annie's Basic Cat Secret

This book is all about my one simple secret to cat behavior. I call it the ABCs of cat behavior (Annie's Basic Cat Secret):

"Cats are like people."

When people are strong, healthy, and confident, they don't feel threatened or intimidated by situations. When people are weak, unhealthy, or insecure, they frequently behave badly. Cats are no different. Like people, they may whine, wet the bed, be irritable, or get mad when they aren't feeling good.

Did You Know? ▪ In the Dark Ages, people were told by the Church to kill cats. For many centuries, cats were thought to be "tools of the devil." Cats almost disappeared from Europe, and as a result the rat population flourished. More than 27 million people—one-third of Europe's population at that time—died from bubonic plague, which is spread by fleas and through rodent feces.

My aim is to help you make your cat stress-tolerant, strong, confident, and happy. It won't cost you much in terms of time and money. A good cat is easy to have if you know the ropes. I will teach you.

Annie's View of Cat Behavior

Diet

Exercise

Environment

Behavior

Before We Begin

A cat's health is important to behavior. None of the advice I give in this book is intended to replace that of a veterinarian. Make sure the cat sees the veterinarian when you have any doubts about his health.

The advice in this book is tailored only to a cat that is spayed or neutered. If your cat isn't, please see Fix 'em Good! (Chapter 5).

Feral Cats

This book also is not meant for feral (wild) cats. It's dangerous to let a feral cat inside your house or to touch one. A feral may never learn to be part of a household. I do not recommend their adoption. There are millions of already tamed cats that will be killed this year due to lack of homes. Alternatives for helping feral cats are listed in the Cat Advocacy section of the Appendix.

Declawing

Declawing is illegal or considered inhumane in several countries. (See Declawing Drawbacks in the Appendix.) It is a risky and painful procedure that amputates the claw, tendon, bone, and ligament to the first knuckle of each joint. While many American veterinarians suggest declawing as a means of alleviating behavior problems such as scratching and aggression, it is, in reality, ineffective.

Declawing at first appears to save time and money. But it undermines the cat's health, confidence, and attitude, and can lead to worse problems. Declawing can make a cat very expensive to own. Owners of declawed cats report higher veterinarian bills, higher home repair bills, and more litter box problems.

Throughout this book, I've included tips on how to offer special treatment for declawed cats. They most definitely need additional help . . . but even the best help will not make up for their loss. Declawed cats often suffer pain and can't truly "exercise." They are forever denied access to muscles they would have strengthened by scratching a post with claws. Loss of muscle mass leads to poor health, stress, and low self-esteem. Pain, attitude, and poor health affect a cat's ability to perform, listen, and behave. *Don't adopt a declawed cat and don't have one declawed.* You are better off with an able-bodied cat, not one that is permanently disabled.

As a cat lover and cat owner consultant, I have moral, ethical, and legal obligations to make only safe and sound recommendations. I will always advise people to never bring home a declawed cat because I know these cats are dangerous and expensive. I would be liable, negligent, and fraudulent to recommend cats that frequently bite people, urinate on sofas, destroy floorboards, and cause the loss of security deposits. *People* are better off owning clawed cats.

Further to that, by adopting a declawed cat you're saying that declawing is okay. Adopting a clawed cat is really a "vote" because you're giving a voice for *your* cat as well as for *all* clawed cats. If you have a well-behaved declawed cat, you will tell others about how wonderful your declawed cat is (and how wrong Annie Bruce was), but are you willing to risk *your* friends, relatives, neighbors, and co-workers and *their* children and furniture to house unhealthy cats that frequently pee and bite? Are *you* willing to risk other people's cats, time, home, children, and money just because your cat happened to triumph over pain, disability, and homelessness? It does not help for you to wait until your cat was declawed and dumped at the shelter for you to cry "but kitty needs a home!" There is no reason why "last resort" cats deserve a *second* chance when millions of clawed cats are still working on their first. *Every* clawed cat needs *your* vote!

The Making of a Good Cat

It really doesn't take much to make a cat happy and well-behaved. The secret to cat behavior is found in these basics.

- A healthy diet
- Exercise and play
- Social interactions
- Touch
- Fresh air and sunshine
- A clean, safe toilet and bed

Solving Problems

No two cases are alike and no single strategy works with every cat, so throughout this book I've included lots of options. Don't feel that you have to try every solution; pick and choose the advice that best suits your set of circumstances, and disregard the stuff you don't think will help. If you get stuck on what to try, think of how you would solve the problem if your cat were a person.

 Cats Are Like People ■ There is no single strategy for solving behavior problems that is effective with every cat or person. We often need to adjust things in many aspects of our life in order to improve our behavior.

Safety

 Just as there are things to do to make a house safe for children, there are steps to take to protect your cat.

Cat Toys

Be sure to keep string and yarn inaccessible. Believe it or not, string can kill a cat. Once a cat starts swallowing string, he can't stop until he chews through it. Cats have been known to swallow very long pieces of string, yarn, or ribbon, causing intestinal blockage and eventually, death.

To ensure your cat's safety, remove any glued-on or removable parts from toys that you give to him. For instance, plastic eyes and noses should be pulled out of fake mice.

Shopping List

✓ cat carrier
✓ curtain cleat or binder clip
✓ tattoo
✓ brightly colored, breakaway cat collar, and a bell
   to use outdoors

See the Products and Resources
section in the Appendix for more
information.

Houseplants Look Enticing But. . .

Cats don't understand that houseplants are not safe to eat. Poinsettias, azaleas, and philodendrons are just a few poisonous and

10

potentially deadly plants. Discourage your cat from playing with any houseplants by saying "No" when he is investigating them. Cover the soil with decorative rocks so that your cat won't be tempted to dig. Hang plants from the ceiling, beyond his reach, or find a new home for plants that are just too tempting.

Cats Don't Always Land on Their Feet

Open windows, balconies, and rooftops are serious hazards for cats. If possible, keep these areas off-limits. If you have lamps on timers, make sure the lamp is secure so that the cat can't knock the lamp over. Otherwise, the lamp is a potential fire hazard.

Don't Wet Him. . . Or Dry Him

Many people use spray bottles as a deterrent for bad behavior, but they can be dangerous. Cats are susceptible to upper respiratory infections, especially if water is forced into the mouth or nose.

Keep the door of the clothes dryer closed when unattended. Every time I close my dryer door, I first look to see that no one's in there.

Be Careful of Chemicals and Cleaners

Mothballs and moth crystals can destroy a cat's liver within a few hours of inhaling the fumes. Use cedar in closets and chests.

Keep your cat away from household cleaners. Anything dangerous for human consumption is often fatal for cats. Use baking soda, vinegar, or environmentally safe natural cleaners instead of commercial cleaning products. Cats are very sensitive to chemicals, so rinse surfaces well after using any kind of cleaner.

After applying fertilizer or weed killer to the lawn, keep your cat inside for the period recommended by the chemical manufacturer and until after the lawn has been watered. Inside the house, use roach and mouse traps instead of chemicals or poison.

The Litter Box

Avoid the use of clumping litters that contain sodium bentonite. The substance has been suspected of killing kittens. Do not keep a litter box in the garage or near a gas-fueled hot water heater, where carbon monoxide might accumulate.

Speaking of the Garage. . .

Antifreeze has been known to kill pets. Garage doors and garage door openers have killed many cats. Warm car engines are attractive on cold nights, and cats often are killed when they are caught unawares beneath a car hood. Before starting your engine, be sure to check for cats.

The Sewing Room, Office, Kitchen, Bathroom

Sewing machine needles and glimmering scissors can seriously injure cats who let curiosity get the better of them. Keep your cat away while you're using the machine.

Cats can swallow rubber bands and other small office supplies. Be sure to keep such items in closed boxes or drawers.

Toothpicks, tinfoil balls, corks, and cellophane can choke cats. Plastic bags can trap or suffocate them. Store these and similar items in closed drawers or cupboards.

Make sure the bathroom is safe for your cat, too. Keep the toilet lid down—a thirsty cat might drink out of the bowl and could be injured by chemicals in the toilet bowl water. He also could be hurt if the seat falls on him. Medicines meant for humans are not meant for cats, so keep them in their containers and out of reach. Aspirin and Tylenol are deadly.

Seasonal Dangers

Cats will chew on or swallow tinsel, Christmas tree water, angel hair, and Easter egg nests, all of which are toxic, so keep a close eye on your cat when you have seasonal decorations in the house. Keep your cat inside during any holidays when firecrackers are used. When the weather is hot, or even just warm, don't leave her in the car. It only takes a few minutes in a hot car to kill your pet.

true story

While cleaning the house one Tuesday morning, I heard Marvin crying loudly. I found him with his leg tangled in the pull cord of the window blinds. He could not free himself because his hind end was hanging about five inches off the floor.

He hissed at me when I went to grab him, but I was finally able to free his leg. I felt lucky that he did not get his neck caught in the cord.

Now I make sure that pull cords are inaccessible by tucking them away or wrapping them around curtain cleats.

Collars, Harnesses, and Leashes

Any cat that is let outside needs a collar with a phone number. Even if your cat is tattooed, he should wear a collar outdoors. Tattooed cats may be okay collarless while indoors, but not outside. Use a bell on his collar when he's outside, but not inside the house; it will drive everyone crazy, especially the cat. Cat collars should fit loosely. Unlike dogs, cats have fragile necks. Cats need to be able to shed the collar to avoid injury should the collar get caught in a fence. Use a breakaway collar made especially for cats. Buy a brightly colored collar so you can spot him easily. Write your name on the collar with a permanent marker or include a tag.

Cats can get out of just about any harness. Use a harness or leash only while you are around to watch. Never leave your cat unattended, even if he's wearing a harness.

Cat Carriers

Use an airline-approved cat carrier, because it will be durable, easily transportable, storable, and washable. Always use a cat carrier when you travel, even in an automobile. It is dangerous to drive with the distraction of a cat loose in a car. I once almost had an accident when my cat got under the brake pedal.

Special Considerations for Declawed Cats

Declawed cats are clumsier and less able to respond to danger than clawed cats. Place padding in areas where your cat may fall. Supervise a declawed cat when you take her outdoors; she won't be able to climb trees to escape dogs and predators, and may have to fight rather than flee.

Don't Lose Him

The best way to permanently register ownership of your cat is to have him tattooed and then register the number with a national pet registry. It is a federal offense for any laboratory to accept a tattooed animal. And unlike a collar, a tattoo can't slip off. (See the Products and Resources section of the Appendix for details.)

true story

A neighbor's cat supervised the loading of a moving van. He had to be flown back from Arizona. Another cat was folded into a reclining chair and loaded onto the moving van. Six weeks later, when his owners took their things out of storage, they found him, barely alive and brain damaged.

You also can use the new microchip implant identification method. Not just any microchip reader can decipher the chip information, but most of them can at least detect that a chip is present. Shelters often have a universal chip reader, but laboratories do not.

The chip is not visible and does not offer the same federal protection that tattooing does, but it can provide additional protection. For more information about getting your cat microchipped, call your local animal shelter or your veterinarian.

For added safety, don't let your cat go outdoors without a collar that has your phone number on it, even if he's tattooed.

Other Dangers

Pet stores carry decals that let firefighters know how many animals are in the house. Firefighters don't have time to rescue your cat, but if they see the decal, they will leave a door open for the cat to escape.

Keep a file of information about each cat in case one of them gets lost. The file should include:

- A few pictures
- Medical records
- The tattoo number, registry address, and phone number
- A written description of the cat

See Chapter 8, Lost and Found, for more information about this subject.

Make Sure She's Not Forgotten

It's a good idea to make provisions for your pet in the event of your death. If a friend or relative doesn't speak up on your cat's behalf, your beloved pet could be sent to a shelter or even sold to a laboratory. Entrust her care to someone you know and trust.

Because animals are possessions under the law, you should include provisions for your cat's care in your will. If you don't have a will, write a letter stating how you want your cat to be cared for. If you have a medical power of attorney, insert a line about what to do with your pet if you become incapacitated. Give the instructions to your best friend or your lawyer.

WARNING ▒ If you are pregnant, do not handle cat litter. There is a risk of toxoplasmosis, a disease that can cause birth defects. Note that toxoplasmosis also can be caused by eating meat that is undercooked or was improperly handled. Ask your doctor and your veterinarian for advice on handling cats when you're pregnant.

Adoption

Adoption is the most fun and the most crucial of all cat decisions. But it's not unusual to bring home a quiet cat and find out that he is really a talker—or, to adopt a cat that was born to jump and be hyperactive when you really wanted one that thought moving from one side of the bed to another was a big trip.

Like people, cats have all kinds of personalities, and each one is unique. Most people cannot live with just any cat. Because each cat is different, it's better to think about the process as a marriage, not an adoption. Although divorce is an option, you want to avoid that by having a thorough, unhurried courtship.

The main goal of this chapter is to help you adopt a cat you are happy with, not just a cat that is happy with you. It will help you reduce the chance of bringing home, and keeping, the wrong cat. And even if you already have a cat, you will find a wealth of general information in this chapter.

> **Shopping List**
>
> ✓ carpet cleaner made for pet stains
> ✓ paper towels
> ✓ video made especially for cats to watch on TV
> ✓ scratching post
> ✓ cat bed
>
> See the Products and Resources section in the Appendix for more information.

Do I Really Want a Cat?

Before you head out to look for a new cat, know what you are getting into. Despite their reputation for being aloof, cats are not animals you can ignore. If you aren't prepared to spend time with them, don't get one.

If you have never owned a cat, you may not realize that cats do certain cat things, and need certain things. New, unsuspecting cat owners may be surprised when they find that their cats regularly:

- *Jump.* Cats like to be in high places (on top of your desk, bookcase, filing cabinet, sofa) to watch people and events and gain information about people behavior.
- *Play.* Cats need interaction with humans. Be prepared to spend time playing with and talking to your cat.
- *Scratch.* Cats have to scratch. Rather than trying to prevent your cat from doing so, train her to use a scratching post and trim her claws regularly.
- *Vomit.* Enough said.

Can I Accommodate a Cat?

Where you live plays an important role in the feasibility of owning a cat, especially if you don't own your own home. Obviously, some landlords do not allow cats, so you'll have to locate apartments that do. If you have Internet access, you can do searches for apartments that allow cats.

Regardless of where you live, you need to think about the following things:

- Does your apartment complex require declawing or require that cats are kept indoors only? If so, you may face litter box problems that could eat up your security deposit and narrow your living options.

- Is your apartment or home big enough for one or more scratching posts or litter boxes? Can it handle more litter boxes if your cat develops an issue with his litter box? (For cats with litter box problems, add one or two *more* litter boxes. Will you have room to add a litter box or two if needed? See Chapter 21, Litter Box Blues.)
- Are you on a quiet street or a busy boulevard? If you live in a congested area, your cat will face increased risks if he goes outdoors.

Where Do I Find a Good Cat to Adopt?

Shelters are unquestionably the best place to find a cat. With thousands of cats being euthanized in your local cat shelters due to lack of homes, adoption is a responsible choice.

Contrary to popular belief, cat shelters don't harbor "rejects." They put cats through adoption tests, so your chance of finding a smart, loyal, and appreciative cat is extremely high in practically any reputable shelter in the country. Kittens younger than eight weeks old often are cared for in a volunteer foster home until they're old enough to adopt. In these cases, the shelter may be able to give you an idea of the kitten's personality and behavior.

What Kind of Cat Do I Want?

At the shelter, you'll encounter strays and unwanted adult cats and kittens that have been put up for adoption. I've had very good luck with stray cats. Even after the stress of being captured, relocated, and caged, strays can be trained to be well behaved.

If you're thinking of owning only one cat, try to find a cat that is used to being alone. This probably will be an adult. If you want a kitten, it's best to adopt at least two kittens so each will have a friend.

There are advantages to adopting an adult cat. While it's hard to know what sort of cat a kitten will become, you'll know whether the size and personality of a grown cat will be suitable for your home or apartment.

If you do adopt kittens, try to get them when they're older than ten to twelve weeks. The longer a kitten stays with her mother, the better your chances of having a healthy, stress-tolerant cat.

Call different shelters to find out if they have older kittens and at what age the kittens were taken from the mother. Find out if the kittens were fostered in a household with children for several weeks. Exposure to children and frequent handling make for a social and loving cat.

Be patient. If a shelter doesn't have what you are looking for this week, it soon will, probably within a month or two. Animal rescue teams are likely to encounter any breed, color, or temperament you want. They can let you know when the exact cat you are looking for arrives.

 Cats Are Like People ■ The essential core personality of any being is unchangeable. No matter how many doctors or professionals we hire, we each have our own desires, which will not budge. We can't love every cat or person we meet. And we definitely cannot live with every cat or person we meet.

Other Ways to Find a Cat

During kitten season (about March to October) and when college semesters end, you can find lots of free cats. Many college students think they want a cat. Later, when they realize they have no place for it during the summer, they surrender it to the shelter or abandon it to fend for itself. Post signs on campus to try to get the cat before he's abandoned.

Newspaper ads are a good resource. And some pet stores allow nonprofit animal rescue shelters to use a section of their store or office to showcase rescued cats.

Fostering is perhaps the best option of all, because you get to live with the cat for a while. Many shelters have fostering programs. You care for their cats in your home until they are ready for adoption. In essence, you get to try out a lot of cats. You'll get to find out if the new cat gets along with your family and current pets. (This is how I ended up taking on a third cat. My foster cat, Marvin-My-Man, got along great with everyone from the moment he arrived.)

Where Not to Get a Cat

Avoid pet stores unless the adoptions are sponsored by a nonprofit agency. Conscientious breeders do not sell kittens or puppies to pet stores. Good breeders want to interview adoption candidates to help find good homes for the pets they've nurtured. Few pet stores put out the effort to ensure a good home.

As I said in the beginning of this book, I do not recommend getting a feral cat. They are difficult and often impossible to train. Some cat owners spend years getting a feral to accept humans.

How Many Cats Do I Want?

Deciding how many cats you can have in your home depends on the space you have available, both indoors and outdoors. It also depends on the amount of time, money, effort, and patience you have for taking care of the cats.

While I cannot predict what the right number of cats is for your situation, I do recommend that you have at least two cats. At the shelter you will meet several cats that get along since shelters nowadays often keep many cats in one room. Cats are social animals by nature. And two cats that get along will groom and play with each other. Some cats are fine having a dog as their social companion. I've even talked to a woman whose pet bird and cat slept and played together for fifteen years!

Owning an Only Cat

If a dog or second cat is out of the question, here are some ways you can help keep your only cat happy.

- Spend as much time as you can playing and being with him. Lure toys, supervised outside walks, and daily massages can really help.
- Help groom him. Pet and scratch your cat often in places he can't lick: his head and neck and under his chin. Groom him more often.
- Leave a light and radio on when you're not home.
- Have a special bed, just for him.
- Provide distractions while you're gone or busy: a bird feeder, TV, or aquarium to watch; safe toys to play with.
- Some videos are made especially for cats and feature birds and wildlife sounds.
- If your only cat will be kept indoors, see the Indoor-Only Cat section in Chapter 19.

For more suggestions on keeping the only cat happy, read *51 Ways to Entertain Your Housecat While You're Out* by Stephanie Laland.

Spotting a Healthy Cat

Cats available for adoption in shelters usually are physically healthy, but you can do your own check for physical and mental health while the cat is still at the shelter. First, pay attention to these things to find out if a cat is interested in being with people:

- When you walk by her cage, does she stand up and try to get your attention?
- Does she stick her paw outside the cage and try to reach for you in a loving way?

If you find one you are interested in, ask the attendant to take the cat out of the cage. As you play with him, observe the following:

- Are his eyes clear, bright, and curious, or watery and half-closed? Does he move his head to watch you? If only his eyes follow you, he may be frightened of his current situation. Or he may just be too frightened to trust anyone for now, and may mellow out once you get him home.
- Does he notice things? Is he playful? Does he hear the snap of your fingers? Take an interest in you or others? Sniff the air? A cat that takes no interest could be very sick or very frightened.
- How does the cat move and walk? Does he purr when you pet him? Does he rub up against you? Does he put his tail straight up when he walks or runs, or when you pet him? These are signs that he is happy to see you.
- Are any fleas, ticks, or ear mites present? Have the shelter help you check for these nasty critters, because body parasites can be very difficult to get rid of, and it may take more than one treatment. However, don't let that prevent you from adopting a cat. (I adopted Sam knowing he had ear mites. I had to treat him for mites about once every five years, and he lived to be more than sixteen years old. The other cats I had at the time never contracted ear mites.)
- Does he talk (meow) too much for you? It's like getting a barker—some people want noisy pets and some don't. Be fore-warned—the cat won't change.
- Is he declawed? My advice is, don't adopt him. Declawed cats are easily stressed, which makes them more difficult to own,

and they usually require more time and money because they are physically challenged. It's also more difficult for them to accept new situations, which means that any changes in a declawed cat's life can trigger health or litter box problems. In some cases, the adoption papers of these cats carry a statement such as "not suitable for homes with children under the age of four" because declawed cats tend to bite more often than do clawed cats.

- Is he sleeping in his litter box? A cat that's sleeping in his toilet could have severe emotional problems unless he is allowed outside so he can pee somewhere else.

- How does he act when he walks by other cats? Does he hiss and growl? Hissing at cats or dogs is okay, but if a cat shows these signs of aggression against people, I'd think twice about adopting him.

- Is the cat responsive to touch? Does he bite you if you pet him gently, or does it take aggressive petting to get him agitated? You may want to avoid a cat that snaps at you too easily. Some clawed cats can have a nervous bite that will go away after a few weeks in your home, but declawed cats aren't as likely to stop biting soon.

- Is he affectionate? Gently stroke his stomach and listen for his purr. Cats who let you rub their stomachs usually trust humans.

Once you've found a cat you like, find out what the shelter already knows about the cat. Look at the adoption papers, which might give you clues as to how the cat will act around other cats, dogs, or children. Usually the papers state how or why the cat ended up in the shelter. If you can, talk to the people who fostered the cat to find out more about its personality and habits.

Finally, like people, each cat has an individual personality that must be respected. You can train him to use a scratching post, but if he's a jumper or a talker, you won't change that. Looks are not enough; fall in love with his personality.

Other Things to Consider

There are many things for you to think about before you make your final decision about adopting a cat. Some of these may seem unimportant now, but keep in mind that owning a cat is a long-term commitment. Making the right decisions now will make life easier and much more pleasant for both you and your cat.

Costs

A "free" cat is never free of expenses. Before you bring a cat home, make sure you can afford to keep him. Adoption fees range from $40 to $120, which should include altering and first shots. These fees do not cover all the shelter's costs. At any price, you're getting a deal while helping your community.

The adoption fee may not include a feline leukemia test, which may cost you $50 or more at the veterinarian's office. If the cost of the adoption and the test seems too high, you may not be able to afford a cat; his upkeep will be much more than these one-time costs. Be aware that you'll also be spending at least $75 per year on cat litter, not to mention the money you'll spend on food, toys, scratching posts, cat beds, shots, and so on.

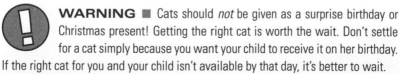

WARNING ■ Cats should *not* be given as a surprise birthday or Christmas present! Getting the right cat is worth the wait. Don't settle for a cat simply because you want your child to receive it on her birthday. If the right cat for you and your child isn't available by that day, it's better to wait.

Your child will appreciate being included to help select the cat. Pick a day when you both can visit a few shelters. Give her an idea of how many different personalities she has to choose from.

Outdoors versus Indoors

As a cat owner consultant, I recommend that people let their cats spend time outdoors. Cats are very smart and can easily get bored when kept inside the house. Time outside helps entertain cats and exhausts both physical and mental energy (curiosity). Adult-supervised outside walks can improve health (sunshine provides vitamin D; chewing grass helps to eliminate hairballs; rolling in dirt cleans fur and skin) and cat safety (for instance, if my husband's blues band leaves the door open, my cats will know how to find their way home). Also, as you'll learn in Chapter 19, supervised walks actually seem to solve most behavior problems in cats.

If you adopt a cat that's used to being outside, you may or may not have a problem with keeping him inside. Adaptability to living indoors-only is dependent on each individual cat, but I have found that most cats benefit from and enjoy time outside.

Male versus Female

Gender is a personal choice. No trait is guaranteed in either sex—it depends more on each individual cat. However, my husband and I both have found that male cats like being held more than female cats do. And we also notice that males have a bit more of a laid-back attitude. But again, no trait is true for *every* male or *every* female.

Spayed female or neutered male cats usually won't spray indoors. When neutered early enough, male cats often won't even spray outdoors, because they were fixed before starting the habit.

Color, Breed, and Hair Length

Siamese are thought of as "talkers" or needy. Of course, not every Siamese has these traits. Tortoise, black, white, calico, tabby, orange—all have somewhat different personalities. You need to check out each individual cat. Just because she's cute or "looks neat" doesn't mean she'll make a neat pet. If you adopt based on color, looks, or breed alone, you may be sorry.

 Cats Are Like People ▨ The more light-hued a cat is, the more vulnerable he will be to the sun's rays—just like we are!

One drawback of the color white: White cats are more susceptible to sunburn, which can lead to skin cancer or other skin problems. As a result, white cats should not be kept outdoors. You can let them out for a short while if you apply a baby-safe sunscreen to her ears and sparsely haired spots on her face and nose.

Hair length can make a big difference in the amount of cleanup and grooming you have to do.

Black Male Cats

Here I will plug my personal choice: Black male cats are the best. They are the smartest and the most lovable and loyal. What's more, black male cats are not in high demand, and smart ones are extremely easy to find. A few shelters even have reduced adoption fees for black dogs or cats. You are likely to be saving a life, because they often are the first to be destroyed.

Returning a Cat

The most common adoption mistake is thinking that just because you brought this cat home he should live with you no matter what. Not all cats fit all cat owners. As the quote at the beginning of this chapter suggests, if you're serious about being a cat owner, "marry" your cat, don't adopt it. We really should "divorce" the ones we don't love, can't trust, or can't stand. Before adopting from any shelter, find out what the return policy is. Make sure you can return a cat up to six months after adoption, as some adult cats take a while to show their true colors in your home.

Because adoption is often traumatic, it can take cats more than two weeks to adjust to a new environment. The adjustment period for adult cats is longer than it is for kittens, so you should keep an adult cat for two months before returning him. Even though a shelter may scoff at your returning a cat, remember that it's you, not the shelter, who has to live with the cat.

true story
Black cats are reputed to be unlucky. But in ancient Egypt, and in Great Britain today, people think black cats bring good luck. I do too.

Foster homes keep cats for as long as three to four months. (One time, I had to keep a foster cat almost six months before she was healthy enough to adopt. She settled into her new home with no problems.) Try not to feel bad about finding another home for an adult cat you've had for a few months.

Kittens are a different story. Try to return a kitten within two weeks if he isn't working out. Kittens have an easier time getting adopted.

If you want to find another home for your cat yourself, tell your friends, advertise in the newspaper, and post signs that you have a cat to give away. Ask a potential owner how she feels about feeding, sleeping with, declawing, and hitting a cat. Will the cat be living outside only? Alone? Set the criteria yourself, because you probably know best what this cat likes or needs. If possible, visit the new owner's home. Ask her to return the cat if things don't work out.

By associating with the cat, one only risks becoming richer.

Colette

The Newcomer

Your new cat's first few weeks in your home is critical. You'll be laying the groundwork for your relationship. And remember, "cats are like people." First impressions are important.

If this is your first cat, get ready for one of life's great pleasures. Cats are great! But they also can be a problem if you go against their grain. This chapter will help get you off on the right foot.

Housebreaking and Confinement

Housebreaking a cat is different from housebreaking a dog. Dogs need to be taught where to relieve themselves (which is outside). From the age of one month, cats naturally use the litter box. "Housebreaking a cat" (at least in this book) means to teach him to use the scratching post and to develop a bond with people.

Confinement is a necessary part of housebreaking. Use a bathroom if you can. It should be large enough to have the litter box at

Shopping List

✓ cat carrier
✓ vitamins
✓ cat food and catnip
✓ food and water bowls
✓ litter box and litter
✓ cat bed
✓ cat toys
✓ scratching post
✓ nail trimmers
✓ bright, breakaway cat collar with bell
✓ kitty oats
✓ radio
✓ night-light (sensor night-light works great)

See the Products and Resources section in the Appendix for more information.

least four feet or so from a "clean" area for his bed, food, water, and scratching post.

If you can't use a bathroom, cover any furniture so the only thing he can scratch is the scratching post. If there's a window, make sure that it isn't drafty and that the cat can't get out of it.

The First Day

Bring the cat home in a carrier. Your new cat may be scared and intimidated by the new situation. Then again, maybe he'll be out happily exploring the house on the first day.

Whatever the case, you don't want to give any cat more than he can handle. To be safe, take him directly to his confinement room or nursery and close the door. It's a good idea to have a wet meal ready before you let him out of his carrier. (Remember, first impressions are important.) The wet meal can be either canned or homemade; see Chapter 12 for more information.

 Helpful Hint ▬ When you choose your cat's name, avoid names that sound like a reprimand. Some cats might not hear the difference between "No" and "Moe."

Have only one person in the room when the cat is first allowed outside the carrier. Another person may overwhelm him, at least during the first hour. When opening the carrier door, speak very gently and encouragingly. Be friendly and sensitive. If he walks toward you, say encouraging words and his name, with pride and joy. To help him get acquainted with the surroundings, show him the wet meal and the litter box. If he runs and hides, don't use his name or say much until he's more relaxed.

Keep his first day as positive, gentle, and quiet as possible by limiting the number of visitors. If possible, sit with him through wet meals and for a half hour to an hour before leaving him alone in his room. By then he'll probably want to nap. Keep a radio on low volume and provide a night-light when it's dark to keep him company.

Helpful Hints

▶ Until your new cat sees a vet, wash your hands after you pet her.

▶ If you have other cats, be sure to give them extra attention during the first month or so of the new arrival, so they don't get jealous.

▶ Place the empty cat carrier in a room where your other cats can check it out. This will acquaint them with the smell of the new cat.

Special Considerations for Kittens

Healthy kittens are always hungry. If yours skips just one meal, call the vet. To help him mature, feed him as many as five wet meals a day.

Start handling your kitten as soon as you get him. Gently pick him up and carry him around. Cuddle him, talk to him. All this contact will domesticate him.

Kittens need to learn right away that they shouldn't bite or scratch bare skin. Even though it might be cute now, it won't be later. Always use a lure toy or other item for playing—not your hands—even on the first day.

You can let your kitten out of the nursery under your supervision as soon as he is litter box trained. Usually this takes no more than a month. Be careful that other pets do not harm him. Don't let him climb curtains or furniture. (For more about playing, see the information about kittens in the Special Considerations section of Chapter 11.) Keep using the nursery until he has learned not to scratch the wrong things. This could take until he's six months old.

If he's an only kitten, keep him in your bedroom at night after he's litter box trained. As long as you aren't and your partner isn't pregnant, let your kitten sleep in bed with you. To prevent smothering the kitten while you're asleep, consider putting his bed directly on top of your bed.

The First Week

Take the cat to a vet for a complete physical and immunization. Shelters generally don't do a comprehensive examination.

Establish good habits right away. Trim his nails as soon as you can. Once the cat is used to his surroundings, have all of your family visit him as much as possible. Wait a few days before introducing other cats or dogs.

To reduce the stress of relocation, include a multivitamin like Tasha's Herbs For Cats (any formula) once a day on a wet meal. Make sure the cat is eating! If not, call the shelter or a vet right away. Call him by his name before serving wet foods during confinement. Say "Here, Louie," for example, even if he's only a foot away. This helps train him to come when called.

Don't let him scratch or bite you even while playing. (See Chapter 20 for help on how to avoid cat scratches and cat bites.)

Start gently handling his feet as soon as possible. If you've adopted your cat from a shelter, most likely you will be able to handle his feet the first day or second day. Your other cats are likely to check out the newcomer through the door. They may talk, reach under the door, and even hiss some of the time. This is good. They are getting used to each other.

After he's used the litter box for a few days, let him out for an hour or so to sniff the house and leave traces of scent around. If your newcomer is shy and likely to hide, temporarily outfit him with bell on a safety release (breakaway) collar so that you can locate him should he decide to run and hide. Lock up your other cats while he's out the first few times.

Once he's using the scratching post, you can let him out for good. You might want to leave his nursery facilities available for him until he's comfortable in the rest of the house.

Start growing "kitty oats" or "kitty grass". (Follow the directions on the package of seeds.) Your new cat probably hasn't had lawn grass to munch on lately. In just a few days he'll enjoy nibbling on fresh green sprouts that provide natural fiber and hair-ball therapy. He is likely to vomit soon after eating the grass so keep nearby the rags or paper towels and carpet cleaner you purchased in Chapter 2.

Introducing the Newcomer to an Older Cat

When the older cat's activities through the door seem more curious and playful than hostile, it's time for him to meet the newcomers. Sometimes this may happen in only one day; sometimes it takes a week. Let the cats meet on a day when you have some time to be around to supervise them. Open the door and let the new cat walk out of his room on his own so that he feels in control of what's happening.

Keep your voice upbeat throughout the cats' initial meeting. Use each cat's name with pride, as long as they're being good. Don't touch either cat when they first meet. If a fight breaks out, stay away until things calm down, and then put the new cat back in his room. (See Chapter 20 for detailed advice about aggression.)

Have a lure toy ready and start playing with all the cats together. This helps relax the atmosphere and make them think "all is normal. . . this is life. . . this is cool." Tell them how great they are for being good.

In seven years, one female cat
and her offspring can theoretically produce 420,000 cats.

*The Humane Society of the United States
(From the Web site www.hsus.org)*

Fix 'em Good!

"Spaying," "neutering," "fixing," and "altering" are terms used
to describe the one medical procedure every cat needs. The
procedure involves removing the sexually functioning parts of your
cat. Female cats are spayed; male cats
are neutered. Neutering removes the
testicles of male cats; spaying is a total
hysterectomy of female cats removing
uterus and ovaries. The reasons for altering are many, and they go beyond the
obvious need to control the number of
unwanted, stray cats. Altering your cat
will, in the case of both sexes, make your
pet less territorial and aggressive. Over-
all, altered cats are better listeners and
they also tend to have longer life spans.

Some owners think it's best to let
a female go into heat, or even to wait
until after she's had her first litter of
kittens, before having her spayed. This is nothing more than an old
wives' tale. With millions of unwanted cats destroyed every year,
and millions more dying from abandonment, there is simply no
reason to let your cat bear a litter of kittens.

Shopping List

✓ locate reasonable priced,
  compassionate veterinarian who performs spay/
  neutering
✓ cat carrier
✓ chicken broth
✓ clean, soft comfortable
  bed
✓ gentle music
✓ night-light

See the Products and Resources
section in the Appendix for more
information.

Some shelters fix kittens as young as two months, but I recommend waiting until a kitten is three months or older and weighs at least two pounds.

An adult cat should be fixed before the shelter lets you take the animal home. If that wasn't done, keep your cat inside until he or she is fixed so that your pet won't contribute to the overpopulation of cats!

Preparing for the Operation

If your cat eats well, relieves herself normally, and is curious and alert, then she's probably ready to undergo the procedure. Call around for prices. One day I called five different places. The quotes for a spaying operation ranged from $26 to $149.

Note your cat's litter box habits. The habits you are observing now should resume within a day after the operation.

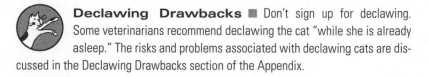 **Declawing Drawbacks** ■ Don't sign up for declawing. Some veterinarians recommend declawing the cat "while she is already asleep." The risks and problems associated with declawing cats are discussed in the Declawing Drawbacks section of the Appendix.

Don't plan to get your cat vaccinated at the same time it's being spayed or neutered. It's a lot for that little body to take all at once.

Understand that if your cat is pregnant when it is spayed, the veterinarian will abort the kittens. Keep in mind that no cat *needs* to have kittens.

After the Operation

Unless complications arise, there's no reason to keep the cat at the veterinarian's overnight. Arrange to pick up your cat late in the afternoon, when she's had time to come out of the anesthesia.

When the cat comes home from surgery, put her in a quiet room with a bowl of water, a soft, warm bed, a litter box, gentle music, and a night-light. She'll probably just sleep the first night, but might welcome some chicken broth and a little company.

 Did You Know? ■ According to the American Humane Association, about 10 million animals are euthanized every year in the United States, most of them because no one will adopt them.

Keep the cat's activities low-key for two or three days after the surgery. Don't entice her into heavy running, jumping, or playing. Keep her indoors for one to two weeks after the surgery to allow the stitches to heal and to lessen the chance of infection in the surgical area. During this period, closely monitor her appetite, temperature, litter box habits, and disposition. Any abnormality could be a sign of infection. Consult the veterinarian immediately if you notice anything unusual. Kittens are especially susceptible to postoperative complications, so monitor their food and fluid intake closely. Some veterinarians tell owners to discourage their cats from licking their genitals for a few days. I just let them lick. Your veterinarian also will give you a list of postoperative care instructions.

Checklist

☑ Make sure that litter box habits are okay now. If they're not, tell the veterinarian.

☑ Have the veterinarian make sure your cat is healthy.

☑ Ask the veterinarian about withholding food before surgery.

☑ Take your cat in the morning, and pick her up in the evening.

☑ Comfort the cat during the next forty-eight hours.

☑ After surgery, check your cat's appetite, keep her indoors, and keep her from jumping.

6 Change Happens

🐾 Family crises and disruptions affect cats, too. Divorce, death, moves, dogs, new members of the household, and even vacations can take their toll on cats by affecting their stress levels. This chapter offers some advice on lessening the strain on your cat when change happens.

As a general rule, whenever there is any major commotion in the household you should try to keep your cat on his usual schedule for eating, playing, going outside, and other regular activities. Give your cat extra attention when you can. Take him for more outside walks.

If you are really in a bind, enlist family members or friends to help you feed and care for him.

Shopping List

✓ radio
✓ cat carrier
✓ *two* bright breakaway cat collars with identification
✓ cat harness
✓ baby powder
✓ catnip toy
✓ spillproof water bowl
✓ flower essence remedy for stress such as Bach Flower Rescue Remedy
✓ health certificate and required vaccinations certificates

See the Products and Resources section in the Appendix for more information.

Moving into a New House

Moving is one of the most stressful situations that people and cats ever face. Before you sign any lease, be sure the new residence allows cats and ask what, if any, conditions there are. Make sure that there are no restrictions demanding that your cat be declawed or kept indoors.

On the brighter side, moving to a new environment also is an opportunity to change your cat's habits. Let's say you want to stop letting your cat out at night; now is the time to do so.

On moving day, put your cat in his carrier or lock him in a bathroom before the movers arrive. Keep your cat confined until the movers have finished loading up their van.

Helpful Hints ▦ To help your cat be more tolerant of change and crisis:
▶ Move furniture around every so often (but don't talk about it to your cat; act as if it's no big deal).
▶ Play loud music on occasion.
▶ Accustom him to traveling in his carrier by taking him on short trips in the car.

When you get to your new house, have food, a scratching post, a litter box, a night-light, water, and a bed set up in a bathroom so that your cat can feel at home as soon as he arrives. Keep him in the bathroom until the movers are gone and the home is secure. Then let him into the main part of the house to investigate. Close off extra rooms for now. If you think you need to let the cat adjust to the new house more gradually, set up a confinement room as described in Chapter 4. If he's really freaked out, shut the door to his nursery when you aren't home. Some cats may hide for a day or two and slowly come out when things settle down. If it's a long move, say in a car crossing several states, he may just sleep for a week, confinement or not (like my Sam did).

Don't let your cat outside for the first few weeks, because he might try to find his way back to his original home. If you do take him outside, watch him closely. Try to make new ground rules for this new yard by teaching him to stay within bounds, as described in Chapter 19.

Talk with your new neighbors. Tell them you have a cat and ask them to call you if the cat ever causes any problem. Give them permission to shoo your cat out of their yard. Chapter 9 has more detailed information for keeping peace in the neighborhood while owning cats.

Dealing with Newcomers (Baby, Dog, Spouse)

Getting a new cat can be a fun, exciting, and rewarding experience. And as the newest member of your household is adjusting to his new surroundings, there are many ways to create a positive atmosphere as your cat becomes part of your family.

A New Baby in the Family

First, remember that a pregnant woman should not handle used cat litter. Call your doctor for advice. If no one else will do it, pay a neighbor's kid to take care of the litter box.

Ask your husband, children, sister, or neighbors to help you look out for the cat, especially while the baby is very young. If possible, start the arrangement before the baby is due so that the cat can begin getting used to the change. Keep your cat's claws trimmed and get him trained on the scratching post. Get him used to these habits before the baby arrives.

 Cats Are Like People ■ Change is difficult . . . especially the older we get.

To get your cat used to noise, play loud music or turn on the TV at a higher-than-normal volume for about an hour. This can be done, fortunately, when you're leaving for an hour or so. And to get the cat used to the smell of baby powder, sprinkle it on a doll or stuffed animal once a day.

In her book, *Twisted Whiskers*, Pam Johnson provides many more tips for dealing with old cats and new babies.

A New Human Member of the Household

Ask the new person to feed the cat and to say the cat's name often. Be patient. Cats must watch and wait to make sure they know "who ya gonna trust?" As your new housemate learns more from you about cats, your pet will learn to trust him or her.

A New Cat

Chapter 4 contains detailed information about introducing a new cat to your household.

true story

When our Bob and Sam first met they had a tremendous fight. It was so fast and quick that, without thinking, I put my hand between them and was scratched.

A year later, Sam and Bob were the best of friends. They slept, ate, and played together for eight years, until Sam died.

A New Dog

Be very careful when bringing a dog into a house with a cat. Some cats simply cannot stand dogs; others love them. If you're getting a new dog or just having one visit, trim the cat's claws beforehand.

If your cat is shy and likely to hide, temporarily outfit him with a bell on a safety release (breakaway) collar. Some cats may hide from a dog for days, and you'll have an easier time finding yours if he is wearing a bell.

When the dog first enters your home, keep him on the leash and confine your cat to the bathroom. After a few minutes, let the dog outdoors to relieve himself. While the dog is gone, let the cat come into the room and smell the area.

Bring the dog back into the house on his leash. Do not hold the cat when they meet; you could get hurt. Be sure that the cat is able to get away and jump high onto something to get away from the dog. This allows him to sniff the air of the room the dog is in and feel safe to observe the dog's behavior. You also can try putting the cat, or the dog, in a carrier and letting the other sniff through the bars for a few minutes. Then remove the loose animal from the room before releasing the one in the cage and letting him sniff the room.

Keep the first contact as pleasant as possible by saying the dog's and cat's names when things are going well. Unleash the dog when you are pretty sure he won't chase the cat. How long that will take depends on the dog, the cat, and the situation.

You might want to make sure that at least one litter box is somewhere the dog can't go. Also, put the cat's food and water bowls out of reach of the dog until they really get used to each other.

Going On Vacation

Taking a trip with your cat can be fun! Last year Mister Lincoln kept me company on a 1,600–mile road trip from Denver to Kanab, Utah. We visited old friends and new dogs at Best Friends Animal Society, the nation's largest sanctuary for abused and abandoned animals. Lincoln and I were guests on Animal Radio, the nation's largest pet talk radio show. We had a blast! But many cats aren't as outgoing or as confident as Lincoln, and there are advantages to leaving your cat at home. Here are tips for going on vacation with or without your cat.

Traveling Without Your Cat

You need to get away from your cat once in a while or you'll go bonkers. Plan on some vacations without him. Arrange for a cat sitter or reserve a boarding kennel. I recommend finding a cat sitter. Being at home is far less stressful for your cat.

Before you leave, put a collar on your cat occasionally, to get him used to wearing it. When you start your vacation, put the collar on and ask the sitter to be sure that it stays on your cat while you're gone.

Stock your house with food and litter. Give your sitter your cat's daily schedule for feeding and play times. Tell the sitter never to let the cat go outside while you are gone. Your cat may freak out when you aren't there, and hide outside.

Show the sitter where your cat likes to sleep, as well as where to find the urine neutralizer, vomit cleaner, vacuum cleaner, water and food bowls, cat toys, and cat carrier. Also give the sitter your veterinarian's phone number and a short written description of your cat. If your cat gets lost while you're away, the sitter can provide this information to the animal control people to help them find your pet. Also give your sitter the phone numbers where you can be reached.

Things to Ask Your Potential Cat Sitter

▶ Are you bonded and insured?

▶ Can you provide a list of references?

▶ What backup plans do you have should something happen to you? Or in the event of bad weather?

Tuck your drapery cords away with a binder clip or something similar. Put away plastic bags or shopping bags with handles (cats can get tangled in bags). Unplug appliances and tuck the cords away. Prop doors open so that your cat can't get locked in a room or closet. (A cat can accidentally push the door shut on himself while playing.) Ask the sitter to leave the radio on while you're gone. Secure a lamp so that it can't tip or be pushed over, and leave it on a timer.

If you have a clawed cat that is not yet trained to a scratching post, and you are really concerned about your furniture, plastic claw covers may be an alternative. They are expensive and may be difficult to fit, but may be an effective temporary solution.

When you get back from your vacation, feed your cat and spend some time with him before checking your message machine or your mail, or unloading the car.

Sample List of Things to Ask the Cat Sitter to Tend to Daily

▶ Feed canned food: Lincoln and Louie get 3 tablespoons of canned food; Bob and Marvin get 1 tablespoon
▶ Refill dry food bowls
▶ Put fresh water in water bowl
▶ Say "Good boy" when you see any cat use the scratching post
▶ Check carpet for vomit; clean spots
▶ Locate each cat; say his name when you find him
▶ Scoop solids from litter box
▶ Play with cats if time permits. Store lure toys away from cats before leaving the house
▶ Water plants
▶ Get mail
▶ Give cats treats right before leaving

Traveling with Your Cat

Most cats would prefer staying home, but if you do have to travel with him, call ahead and make sure your hotel allows cats. Ask if there are any restrictions or is there a deposit required.

If you're traveling by air, you must have a ticket, an airline-approved cat carrier, and a health certificate and proof of vaccines signed by your veterinarian for your cat. Call the airlines to find out what else may be required. Outfit your cat with *two* breakaway collars just in case he accidentally gets out of the carrier. If you're traveling by car, always use a cat carrier. It can help protect your cat in case of an accident and prevent him from distracting you while you drive. Include a catnip toy and a towel or blanket.

Helpful Hint ▦ Avoid shipping your cat by airplane if at all possible. It's very stressful and somewhat dangerous if they are put in the cargo area. Cats with short noses, such as Persians, could have trouble breathing in the limited oxygen of cargo areas. If the airline allows it, it's better to keep your cat with you in the passenger section and take a direct flight. A catnip-filled toy or dried lavender in a sack may help your cat deal with flying.

Don't ever leave your cat locked up in the car for more than a few minutes. In warm weather, don't leave him in the car at all. It takes less than three minutes for a car to get to 100 degrees on a warm day. A hot car will kill him.

Whatever your mode of travel, bring water and food. Some pet stores sell water bowls that collapse or won't spill. Also carry a small litter box. Periodically put it on the floor for him to use, and then store it in a plastic bag. And at all times during the trip, make sure your cat wears a collar (or even two!) AND a harness. Write your name and phone number on both.

WARNING ▦ Tranquilizers are *not* recommended for pets traveling on airplanes. Your cat may get so relaxed he could stop breathing.

Shipping Cats Via Service

Many companies specialize in transporting pets across the country or around the world. Here are two that caught my eye while searching the Internet:

PetTransporter Worldwide offers complete service for flying your pet in the United States or around the world. They will pick up your cat at your house and take him to the airport. They will let you know everything you need to know concerning transporting your pet—including paperwork, immunizations and quarantine required in other countries. Your cat will fly in a carrier placed in a human-grade pressurized and climate-controlled area directly under the pilots' cabin. Call PetTransporter Worldwide at 1-800-264-1287 or visit *www.pettransporter.com.* For people who don't like their cat on airplanes, there is a road pet transporting company that services the continental United States. Pro-Pet-Transports relocates pets via driving only—no flying. Cats and dogs are transported in the luxury of a mini-pet mobile. Pro-Pet-Transports provides personal attention for each pet. Call Pro-Pet-Transports at 1-866-273-7387 or visit *www.pro-pet-transports.com.*

With the qualities of cleanliness, discretion, affection, patience, dignity, and courage that cats have, how many of us, I ask you, would be capable of being cats?

Fernand Méry

Litter Boxes Etc.

🐾 This chapter discusses litter, litter boxes, the best locations for the litter box, and what you'll need to maintain your cat's "bathroom." (Note: If your cat has a litter box problem, please refer to Chapter 21.)

Litter Types

There are many types of litter on the market. And every week it seems, there is a new type of cat litter on the shelf. Most litters are disposable; some are even flushable. Clawed cats are not likely to care what type you use. Declawed cats, on the other hand, often are challenged with litter box issues. Even years after surgery, a declawed cat could resist changes to her litter box routine.

Nonclumping Clay Litters

Granulated pieces of clay litter are about the size of small-grain rice. Litters that are 100 percent clay are natural, very inexpensive, and available in every grocery store and pet store across the country. They have been on the market since 1945.

Note that clay litters aren't biodegradable or flushable. The clay naturally contains silica dust, which is a known carcinogen. The manufacturers say that cat litter doesn't have any more silica dust than do sandy beaches. Even so, if your cat has a sensitive health or behavior problem, you may want to try biodegradable litters. Many, such as alfalfa pellets, are dust-free and flushable.

Some clay litters are scented with a deodorizer that absorbs odors or is activated when the litter is pawed at or stirred. Your cat may or may not like the scent, so try both kinds.

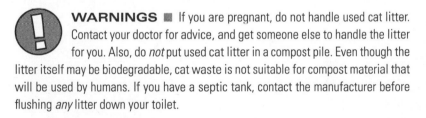

WARNINGS ▮ If you are pregnant, do not handle used cat litter. Contact your doctor for advice, and get someone else to handle the litter for you. Also, do *not* put used cat litter in a compost pile. Even though the litter itself may be biodegradable, cat waste is not suitable for compost material that will be used by humans. If you have a septic tank, contact the manufacturer before flushing *any* litter down your toilet.

Clumping Clay Litters

Clumping litter, also known as "scoopable," forms a solid ball when urine penetrates a deep layer of the litter. The urine hardens the litter, which then can be scooped out in a hard ball. This litter lasts longer and controls the smell of urine quite well. Some declawed cats may prefer the fine texture and softness of clumping litters.

Because clumping litters control the odor so well, they seem ideal at first, especially if you have more than one cat. But there is a serious problem with some clumping/scoopable litters. For clumping litters to work, they need a clumping agent. A popular clumping agent in many scoopable brands is sodium bentonite. This agent acts as a cement and may compromise your cat's health. An article written by Marina McInnis for *Tiger Tribe*, a now defunct holistic cat magazine, detailed the author's experiences with clumping litters containing sodium bentonite. After losing four litters of Japanese Bobtail cats, she determined that the kittens' deaths were caused by the sodium bentonite. After changing the litter, she no longer had the problem. The difficulty can be traced to sodium bentonite's properties. It expands to fifteen times its size when wet. When a cat steps in the litter box, some sodium bentonite clings to her paws. Later on, the cat will lick it off. Once it gets into her digestive system, this trace residue will expand. According to McInnis, this results in an impaired immune system, respiratory distress, and irritable bowel syndrome. Nonclumping clay litters at least have larger granules, which tend to fall off of cats' paws. And they don't contain this type of cement, which gives scoopables their "clump."

WARNING ▓ Clumping/scoopable litters containing sodium bentonite may kill kittens. Avoid litters containing sodium bentonite. If your cat is extremely young and has a medical condition or behavior problem, you'll want to make sure the litter isn't contributing to his problems.

Manufacturers do not have to disclose ingredients on the litter's label, so you'll have to call them and ask if the clumping litter you use contains sodium bentonite. If it does, try another brand. If you really want a litter that is soft and will clump somewhat, try SWHEAT, Here's The Scoop! and World's Best Cat Litter. They may not clump as hard, but they *do* clump and are flushable and biodegradable.

While biodegradable clumping litters are safe for both cat and plumbing, litter containing ingredients such as calcium bentonite, agar, and sodium bentonite may ruin the plumbing in your house. *Some municipalities may fine you if certain clumping litters are found in your pipes or sewer.*

Biodegradable Litters

"Biodegradable" means that the litter will break down by the action of little bugs eating it at the city dump. Even though clay and newspaper litters are natural, they don't "break down" in the city dump.

Helpful Hint ▧ A friend told me that rabbit food can be used as cat litter. It's not only pretty cheap; it also clumps a little bit.

Biodegradable litters come from plants. These litters are made of alfalfa, corncob, aspen, citrus peels, pine, and wheat. Most are flushable, but call the manufacturers to be sure, especially if you have a septic tank. New biodegradable litters are hitting the market almost every year. Some litters are finely ground; others are more like pellets. Some (SWHEAT, Here's The Scoop! and World's Best Cat Litter) clump naturally, without sodium bentonite. Most are dust-free.

Just a Few Biodegradable Cat Litters ▧ For contact information, see the Products and Resources section of the Appendix.

▸ CatWorks The Premium Cat Litter: plant-based pellets
▸ SWHEAT SCOOP Wheat Litter: wheat based, soft, clumps, flushable
▸ World's Best Cat Litter: soft, clumps, flushable
▸ Here's The Scoop! Clumping Cat Litter: not flushable, clay based, natural clumping agent of guar gum
▸ Rabbit food pellets (alfalfa pellets sold for rabbit food can be found at feed stores): clumps somewhat, flushable
▸ Feline Pine: 100 percent kiln-dried southern yellow pine

Newspaper Litters

Litters recycled from newspaper come in pellet and sand-type form. These are found in grocery stores and pet stores. But newspaper could be toxic to some cats or people because some inks are toxic. Some of these litters also don't control odor too well; however, my cats like finely, ground (non-pellet) newspaper cat litters. I add Mother Nature's Odor Remover for odor control.

Litter Boxes

Look for litter boxes at hardware stores, pet stores, and yard sales. Disinfect and rinse them well before using.

Have at least one box per cat. Add an additional box if your cats are kept indoors-only or are declawed.

The size of the box depends on the cat and his personality. If your cat is big or likes to fling litter around, consider a bigger litter box. Declawed cats and other handicapped cats tend to require a larger box for better balance.

When adding a new litter box, consider that a cat may not use the new box for a few days. Don't force him into it. Don't put him inside it. Sound positive when he gets near it, and let him accept it on his own terms.

Covered Litter Boxes

Covered boxes help keep the litter and the smell contained and hidden. Some cats, however, don't like the cover. Covered boxes generally are too small. If you're going to get one, get as large a box as you can.

A covered box might leak unless the top has a locking lid and an inside lip. Scooping out solids is more inconvenient, because you have to deal with these extra parts.

If you get a litter box with a swinging door, be prepared to remove it. You may have to, because some cats like to stick their head out of the box while relieving themselves.

Uncovered Litter Boxes

Uncovered boxes are easier to maintain. They come in different sizes and shapes, though most are rectangular. A few models have a "lip," which is claimed to keep down mess. You also can use plastic utility bins, which are widely available at hardware and discount stores, as litter boxes. If you get them, though, don't use anything taller than twelve inches, because it will be too high for your cat. There also is a triangular box made especially for corners, which works quite well for smaller areas. These are very easy to clean and handle.

Litter Box Locations	
Good Locations	*Bad Locations*
Anywhere your cat can see who's coming	Around the corner or behind things
Laundry room, bathroom, utility room, basement	Near food, water, scratching posts, beds, or play areas; living rooms, dining rooms, kitchens, bedrooms, and areas where the family likes to relax; garages and places near furnaces and gas-fueled water heaters, where carbon monoxide could collect, or where it's not pleasant to be
Every level of the house where the cat spends time	Remote, dark places; basement-only litter boxes
One box per level for sick, declawed, old, or very young cats	One location only or outside only; physically challenged cats need additional help
Quiet places with some privacy; if possible, out of dogs' reach	Where dogs or others may torment or scare the cat while he uses it
Lighted and pleasant places; put a nightlight nearby	Dark and uninviting places
On linoleum, tile, or wood floors; or use a nonporous office floor mat or piece of cardboard over your carpet; a surface that is easy to clean	Directly on the carpet—when he reaches outside the box to scratch the litter, he can snag or claw at the carpet

High-Tech Boxes

There also are electronic, self-cleaning litter boxes available that automatically remove the solids. One model even senses the cat entering the litter box. A few minutes after he leaves, a mechanical part rakes across the clumping/scoopable litter recommended for these models, and places the clump in a disposal tray.

While it's convenient, the manufacturers warn that the motor starts automatically and that children, hands, and clothing should be kept away from it. As with anything automated, be careful.

In addition, some cats are frightened of automated devices. Just one scare may be enough to stop a cat from using his box. A 30-day guarantee may not be a long enough trial period for your cat. This is a very expensive box that won't be any good if your cat stops using it.

Litter Maintenance

Always read the package and follow the manufacturer's recommendations for the litter you're using.

With clawed cats, you should be able to get by with scooping solids once a day. For declawed cats, inside-only cats, or cats with litter box problems, scoop solids and wet spots more often. Be careful about sudden changes in litter brands, boxes, and locations.

Take the poop outside the house as soon as you lift it out, because it will stink up your garbage and house. Or, if the litter is biodegradable and flushable, flush it down the toilet.

Clay litter or nonclumping litter usually starts to smell in about a week. Dump, wash, and thoroughly rinse the box; cats are very sensitive to household cleaners.

Leave an odor bag, such as those available from Mother Nature's Odor Remover (see the Products and Resources section of the Appendix) or an open box of baking soda near the litter box area to absorb odors.

Be sure to thoroughly wash your hands after handling litter boxes or litter.

 Helpful Hints ■ Wash the box every week. This formula has worked well for me:

2+ parts natural orange oil all-purpose cleaner (found in health food stores)
1 part chlorine bleach (optional—I occasionally add chlorine)
10 parts water

Put ingredients in a spray bottle. This solution is good for washing litter boxes as well as washing kitchen counters to prevent germs from spreading.

It's cat urine, not cat poop, that eventually overwhelms the litter. By spooning the wet spots out, you can lengthen the life of the litter. However, if you are lazy, as I am, and you live in a dry climate, stirring the wet spots into the rest of the dry litter also will help keep odors down. This allows the urine to soak into the rest of the litter.

Maintaining Nonclumping Clay Litters

If you use nonclumping clay litters, fill the box one-half inch to two inches deep with five to ten pounds of litter. (Some manufacturers recommend levels as deep as three inches, but my cats like lesser amounts.)

After lifting the solids, shift and shake the litter box so that one-third to one-half of the litter box is exposed. Many declawed cats, and some clawed cats, prefer stepping on bare plastic rather than on gravel.

To reduce dust clouds, don't pour the litter. Instead, let it slowly slide out of the bag or box into the litter box.

Maintaining Clumping Clay Litters

Getting clumping or scoopable litters to work properly usually requires maintaining a certain depth. This means you add litter as the level of litter drops. If you use clumping litter, read the package for instructions on how to maintain the litter box, and when to empty and wash it.

Maintaining Biodegradable Litters

Read the package for instructions. Some biodegradable litters may require you to use more litter up front, but they tend to last longer and don't need to be changed as often—you can simply add more litter after taking solids out. Most are safe to flush. Call the manufacturer to be sure.

 Helpful Hints ■ Other uses for 100 percent natural, nonclumping clay litters:

▶ Garage spills—absorbs oil or grease
▶ Charcoal grills and BBQs—protects bottom of grill and absorbs grease
▶ Trash cans—a layer in the bottom reduces odors
▶ Refrigerator—absorbs odor
▶ Closets, storage areas, and boats—absorbs musty odors and moisture
▶ Snow and ice—sprinkle on sidewalks and steps for traction
▶ Facial mud pack—mix unscented natural clay with a little water, smear on face, let dry and rinse off

Special Considerations for Declawed Cats

When a cat is declawed, a veterinarian will recommend a special litter for a couple of weeks after surgery. He will sell you an expensive, dust-free, paper-based, sterile litter made for postoperative care of declawed cats. *But just because there is a special litter designed for declawed cats doesn't mean the cat will use it. Some cats stop using a litter box altogether after being declawed.*

Once a cat is declawed, he's at higher risk of getting infected paws, which will require more operations. Keep inspecting his toes once a month to check for infection. Again, it's best to avoid facing unnecessary litter box challenges by not declawing any cat.

A Word About Toilet Training

Cats can balance enough to use the toilet. It's a great way to reduce litter wastes. If you want to give it a try, you'll find each step described in *How to Toilet-Train Your Cat: 21 Days to a Litter-Free Home,* by Paul Kunkel.

Switching Brands of Litter ▪ If you need to change brands of litter, set up another box with the new litter to see if your cat will use it. Avoid making a sudden change. You'll need to make sure your cat will use the litter before switching all litter boxes in the house to the new brand. Beware: If a cat suddenly stops using a litter that she's been using with no problem, she could be very sick. See Chapter 21 for help.

Lost and Found

A lost or found cat situation is very stressful. Here are tips to prevent the problem and to help solve it should it happen.

Prevention

Even the most cared-for cat may get lost. These are steps you can take beforehand to make him easier to find.

Shopping List

✓ breakaway collar with identification
✓ tattoo
✓ microchip implant
✓ poster board
✓ markers
✓ staple gun, nails, or tape
✓ fliers

See the Products and Resources section in the Appendix for more information.

- Get him a bright, reflective collar with your phone number written on it. Or include a tag. A cat without a collar and phone number is very hard to identify, which significantly decreases your chances of finding him. Keep a collar on him even if he's an indoor-only cat.

- Get your cat tattooed. Fifty percent of all tattooed cats that are reported lost are recovered. (Tattooed dogs have a 99 percent return rate.) See Products and Resources in the Appendix for information about the tattoo registry.

- Get your cat a microchip implant (call your veterinarian or local shelter).
- Let your neighbors know that you own a cat. Your cat could be taken to the pound if people don't know that he belongs to you.
- Take your cat on supervised outdoor walks so he can get to know the area a little better. Train him as described in Chapter 19. Should he accidentally be let outside, he'll have a better chance of knowing what to do until someone lets him back in.
- When outside, do not trust a harness to restrain him. Use a cat carrier if the cat really must be restrained outside. A cat can slip out of a harness almost as easily as he can slip from your sight.
- Don't complain to your neighbor if his dog chases your cat and no injury or misfortune results. It's a valuable lesson for your cat to be on guard while outdoors. Provide a safe place where your cat can jump or climb to safety.

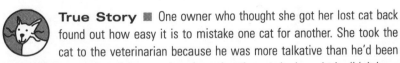

True Story ■ One owner who thought she got her lost cat back found out how easy it is to mistake one cat for another. She took the cat to the veterinarian because he was more talkative than he'd been before. That was when the owner found out that the cat she brought in didn't have the same dental work that her own cat had. She was lucky. She not only found the real owners of the cat she'd thought was hers; she also got her own cat back a couple of weeks later.

- Keep your cat inside on any holiday that involves firecrackers. Shelters report a rise in lost animals during the holidays. A cat can become disoriented by the unusual noise and commotion.
- Keep a picture and description of your cat on hand. Many cats look alike.
- Make sure your cat is spayed or neutered, and feed him right. Well-fed, altered cats stay closer to home.

How to Find a Lost Cat

Fear, worry, and illness can overwhelm you if you lose your cat. Try to eat something, remain calm, and visualize a positive outcome. Your cat wouldn't want you worried sick. To increase the chances of finding her, there are steps you can take as soon as you discover your cat is gone:

- *Act fast.* Begin searching as soon as you know your cat is missing. The sooner you canvass the area, the more likely it is that people will remember seeing her.
- *Ask parents if their children can help find your cat.* Children often are better at spotting stray animals. Describe your cat and leave your phone number so they can call if they see her.

 Cats Are Like People ■ Lost cats get confused, just as lost children do. They miss their homes and family and being fed and don't know how to care for themselves.

- *Fill out a missing-cat report at your local shelters.* Visit each shelter regularly and look at impounded strays. Don't depend on someone at the desk to check—you need to go to see for yourself. Also, visit the shelters in surrounding areas. Just because you lost the cat in your own city doesn't mean that she will not be found elsewhere.
- *Advertise in the Lost and Found section of your local newspapers.* Describe the cat and include the area and the date she was lost.
- *Check the newspaper ads for found cats.* Answer all ads that have similar descriptions, even if the sex is wrong.

 Warning! ■ Do not include your name or address on any "Lost Cat" advertisement, poster, or flyer. People may try to scam or hurt you. Do not respond to ads alone; take along a friend and let others know where you both are going.

- *Print and post signs in the area where you lost her.* Make fliers with your cat's picture, your phone number, the date you lost her, the vicinity, and any applicable reward. If the cat was lost from your house, post signs throughout the neighborhood as soon as possible so that residents know you are worried. Sometimes someone may find a cat and not turn it in to the shelter just to see if anyone cares enough to post a "lost cat" sign. Ask local grocery stores and gas stations to let you display your signs there.
- *Sometimes local radio stations will make an announcement* about your lost cat if you call them.
- *Don't give up.* Some cats find their way home after a few days. Some cats even show up months later.

true story

When Sam was about seven years old, we took him with us on a fishing trip, just a few miles from home. Sam slipped out of his harness (fortunately, I had a collar on him as well). He was missing for five horribly long days. Sam was found because we had left a flier at a building near the last place he was seen. We finally got a phone call early one morning—one of the workers had spotted a black cat in the building, wearing the red reflector tag on his collar. When we arrived, I called "Sam" three times, and he emerged from behind a stack of pallets in the basement.

Sam usually doesn't have much to say, but on that drive home, he talked a lot. He had lost one pound and had a minor cold but was so happy to see me. I got him tattooed soon after this happened and never took him fishing again. He didn't mind.

When You Find a Lost or Stray Cat

When you find a cat, it is very difficult to distinguish whether he's a feral (wild) cat, one that's just cruising the neighborhood, or truly lost. Unless the cat has identification, or you've been trained with cats, or you've witnessed his entire daily routine, you won't really know. If you really think he's lost:

● Don't touch a strange cat or take a lost cat home with you unless it is in obvious and exceptional need. A cat can seriously hurt you. Unless you are trained to handle cats, stay away. Contact your local shelter and report the stray.

● If you do end up with a found cat, call the local shelters to find out if they have descriptions of lost cats. Let them know you have a found cat.

Did You Know? ■ Unless they have been taught hunting and survival techniques, cats seldom know how to fend for themselves. Hunting is not instinctive in most domestic cats.

● Post fliers and advertise in local newspapers that you found a cat. Include where he was found, what he looks like, and how to contact you.

● Read the Lost and Found ads for cats matching his description.

● If no one claims the cat, either find another home for him or turn him in to the local shelter.

true story

Simon was my second black cat, and very loyal. When he was nine years old, he disappeared. It was not uncommon for him to leave for two weeks in the dead of the iciest Detroit winters. But one winter he disappeared and showed up on our back porch thirteen months later. He walked into the house as casually as if he'd been gone overnight.

My mother and I confirmed it was Simon because of his torn right ear and an ulcer on his left front leg. We always wondered where he was all those months. He never did tell us.

We all have enough
strength to bear the
misfortunes of others.

François de la Rochefoucauld

Neighbors

🐾 Neighbors can be wonderful! We can share common interests in cats. We can help each other when we go on vacation, taking care of cats and mail and so on. But not all encounters with neighbors are positive experiences. Our cats can sometimes cause us to interact with neighbors in ways we'd rather not. Occasionally our cats do something—or our neighbors or their pets do something—that causes conflict.

Shopping List

✓ landscaping netting
✓ pine cones or rocks
✓ ammonia or vinegar
✓ bright, breakaway collar with bell

Optional

✓ electronic deterrents
✓ electronic fences
✓ fence guard
✓ outdoor kennel

See the Products and Resources section in the Appendix for more information.

Keeping Peace in the Neighborhood

Cats are very social creatures. They like to hang out with others and often wander into neighbor's yards. Here are tips for keeping peace with your neighbors.

Your Cat

If your cat goes outside and likes to visit your neighbors, here are some things you can do to let neighbors know that you are a responsible cat owner:

- Whenever your cat goes outside, put a very bright breakaway collar on her. Make sure that your phone number is on the collar, and add a bell. The collar will let others know that your cat is not a stray, and the bell warns birds as well.
- Feed your cat well. A well-fed cat is not likely to roam much.
- Train your cat to stay in your yard (see Chapter 19), stop letting her outside, or restrict her outdoor access to the daytime only. (The less your cat roams unattended, the less conflict you will cause in the neighborhood. Cats prowl more at twilight, when birds and mice come out.)

true story

There was a biscuit factory in England that was losing thousands of dollars' worth of food to mice. The owners tried everything—poison, traps, even hunting dogs. But the dogs ate more biscuits than they saved. When all else failed, a dozen cats were brought in. Within two weeks, all the rats and mice were gone and the factory inventory was saved!

- Put water and a bird feeder in your backyard to keep your cat inside her own area.
- Praise your cat when she brings home mice, but say nothing about birds. Don't yell at your cat for killing prey, because that will only confuse her. It's natural for cats to bring home their food or live cat "toys." Quietly dispose of any prey when she's not looking. Feeding more natural or raw foods may cut down on the amount of prey she brings home.
- Get to know your neighbors. Tell them that you own a cat and that you don't like your cat going into other people's yards. Give them permission to scare your cat should she go into their yard. Give them your phone number and tell them to feel free to call. Avoid making them afraid of you, which would make them more likely to call the police or animal pound instead of calling you.

● If a neighbor complains to you, be sympathetic. Tell him you understand his frustration, apologize, and promise to do something about it. Then follow through.

Did You Know? ■ A study of feral cats found that birds constituted just 4 percent of the cats' diet.

▶ Ninety percent of birds escape cat attacks, but only 20 percent of mice escape.

▶ Mouse "squeaks" are at the sound and frequency that cats hear best.

▶ It's been proven that better-fed cats make better mousers.

The Neighbor's Cat

Cats like to be with cool people. If someone else's cat likes to hang out with you and your cat, it's because he thinks you are neat. But there are things to consider when it comes to neighborhood cats:

● If a neighbor's cat is hanging around, either tell him to go away each time, or let him hang around as long as he doesn't start trouble. If you let him hang around, give attention to your cat only. This helps let your cat know that the strange cat is not really important in your life. She'll have no reason to be jealous. Don't touch a strange cat or let one inside your house—strange cats often won't leave.

● If a neighbor's cat is coming into your house through the cat door, you may need to surprise or squirt him sometime to scare him out of the house. Close the door when you are not at home to watch. It's best to avoid the use of cat doors because they allow a cat to come and go as she pleases, which can cause more problems. But if you *must* have a cat door, there are special magnetic doors and collars that will allow only your cat to go in and out. There is a big drawback with that kind of door—if the cat loses the collar, she won't be able to get back in.

- Don't complain to your neighbors about little things, such as their cat coming into your yard. Unless a situation is very serious, complaining often solves nothing and makes matters worse. It's best not to complain about a dog that seldom chases your cats, because accidents do happen, and besides, occasionally upsetting your cat can make her more respectful of her outdoor privileges.

true story

My neighbor's big gray cat, Gray Baby, comes into our yard every day. I like him to, because he's so big that he's very effective in keeping all other cats away. And he reminds my cats that they are not the only cats in the world.

My cats (minus Lincoln) and Gray Baby will lie out on the patio together, in peace. Gray Baby knows not to cause any trouble because anytime he does, I shoo him away for a day or two. As long as he's acting civilized, he can visit with my cats anytime.

Deterrents/Guards

There are several ways to deter cats from getting into yards or gardens. There also are things that you should never use for this purpose.

- Bury landscape netting below the surface of loose dirt to prevent cats from using the soil as a litter box. They'll get their claws caught and won't want to dig there. Pine cones and decorative rocks also can help.
- Don't use mothballs; the fumes can permanently damage cats' kidneys. White onions or orange peels work for a short while. No cat owner has reported to me that store-bought spray deterrents/repellents have been effective for use outside.
- If your cat is using a child's sandbox as a litter box, cover it when the children are not playing in it. Try putting a litter box outside in your yard.
- Sprinkle ammonia or vinegar in the garbage before putting it out. This may deter cats, but probably won't stop dogs or raccoons.

● If there is a special area of a yard that all cats must stay out of, try one of the electronic choices on the market. Sonar devices that emit sound waves as a deterrent have mixed results. A motion-activated sprinkler may be more effective. I haven't tried these, but both the price and concept seem reasonable. One popular brand is The Scarecrow by Contech Electronic Inc. See the Products and Resources section in the Appendix for more information. Although I strongly discourage squirting a cat in the face with water, if a cat is on the verge of being killed by a neighbor for trespassing, this may be a fairly inexpensive alternative. Position the motion activated sprinkler so that it comes on when the cat gets near the property line, and this can help with keeping your cat in the yard.

 Helpful Hint ■ If there is a spot in your yard (or your neighbor's yard) that you would like to protect from cats' spraying, try a wide layer of pine cones or decorative rocks.

● A fence guard is a wire netting that attaches at the top of a fence. It's U-shape is designed to keep cats inside the yard. The cat can still climb the fence but the fence guard will prevent your cat from jumping over the top. Ads for fence guards often are found in the back of cat magazines, but you can ask your local pet stores and fencing companies about them too.

● Electronic fencing, also known as an "invisible" fencing, can help to keep a pet in the yard, but it should be used as a complement to outside training, not as a substitute for it. The "fence" is installed by burying a wire along the perimeter of the property. The cat then wears a special device on his collar that the wire will detect. As the cat approaches the property line, the collar may vibrate and then emit a shock if the cat continues to walk toward it. Others just shock. Some models may require a special adapter to tone down the severity of the shock so that it's suitable for a cat. Manufacturers recommend that you teach your cat what the yard boundary is first, before you begin the vibration and shock treatment. It's cruel to just install a shocking device with no warning to the cat. That said, if you don't approve of using shock treatment to train your cats, it's very cheap and easy to train a cat to stay in the yard *without* installing expensive electronic gadgets. I don't recommend spending a lot of money on cat training, period. A good electronic fence can be very expensive. Don't settle for something cheap or you may not like the results. Call different companies. Ask what kind of guarantee they have, and how safe their product is for *cats*.

- Another option is to install a chain-link cat kennel. Make it so the cat can access it from the house by way of a cat door. Your cat can't roam, but she can still get fresh air. Put in an outdoor cat tree, shelves, or a dog house if you can. Add a padlock to help keep it secured.

- A dog will usually keep a cat out of its yard. Buy one for your neighbor. (Yeah, right!)

true story

A neighbor came to me one day and said he knew that the neighborhood cats were using his flowerbed for a litter box. He wanted to warn me that he didn't like the smell and was going to call the humane society and have traps set.

I thought about it for a few minutes, and then offered to buy him some new soil to repair the damage that the cats had caused. I realized that at least one of my cats probably was contributing to his problem.

When I acknowledged the problem and offered a solution, his attitude changed. He decided not to have the traps put out, kindly refused my offer to pay for the soil, and turned out to be a really nice neighbor.

But I got a cat kennel anyway and trained my cats to stay in the yard.

Most beds sleep up
to six cats. Ten cats
without the owner.

Stephen Baker

Cat Beds

Shopping List

*Optional stuff—cats will
sleep on practically anything,
anywhere, anytime.*

✓ fleece fabric or blanket
✓ clean cotton pillow case
  with folded towel inside
✓ old, clean down coats
✓ cardboard box with old,
  clean blanket

See the Products and Resources
section in the Appendix for more
information.

Cats sleep about sixteen to eighteen hours a day, depending on their age, health, physique, and personality. If neither you nor your partner is *not* pregnant, it's okay to have a cat sleep in your bed, but your cat having his own bed has its advantages, too. Comfortable, easy-to-clean cat beds in fun locations can help your cat feel secure, help control cat hair, and make it easy to know where he is most of the time.

true story

Noise does not prevent some cats from sleeping. My husband, who played in a rock 'n' roll band years ago, once had a cat that would climb into the band's bass drum. The cat would sleep inside the pounding drum for hours while the band practiced for their next performance.

Types of Cat Beds

Different cats prefer different types of beds. Some cats prefer wide-open flat beds such as a pillowcase with a blanket inside, while others prefer a doughnut-shaped bed that provides support while they're curled up.

Before you invest in a cat bed, make sure it's easy to clean. Can it be washed by hand or in a regular machine, or does it need commercial laundering? Cats prefer clean beds and will stop using one if it's dirty, so you'll need to be able to keep it clean easily.

Brand-new beds cost anywhere from $10 to $60. You can get nearly new ones at yard sales, your local animal shelter's rummage sales, or thrift stores for just a few bucks. Or you can make one.

Did You Know? ■ A cat's body temperature falls slightly when she sleeps. Many cats will change napping locations to follow the sun.

Because many cats love to sleep on a clean, nicely folded piece of fleece fabric, buy a yard or two at the fabric store. (Fleece fabric usually is on sale in December and January, but check at other times too.) To keep cat hair down, fold the fabric several times over so it fits on top of a pillow or inside a box. Every week or so, refold it so that a clean side is exposed. Every month, throw it into the washing machine. Because fleece is fast-drying, line dry it rather than putting it into a clothes dryer. During hot months, slip the folded fleece into a cotton pillowcase for a cooler bed.

You can also make cat beds out of old down-filled coats. Or simply use a cardboard box lined with a clean old blanket.

If your cat quits using a bed that he previously liked, it's probably dirty. Air it out outside for a day in the wind and sun, or wash it in very mild detergent and rinse it well. You also can try moving the bed or placing it at a different height, just in case it's in a draft or he wants a change.

Cats Are Like People ■ Cats like clean, warm, safe, and dependable beds.

Locations for Cat Beds

Try different locations and different heights—some cats want to be as high as possible. Keep the cat bed near food, water, and scratching posts, but have the litter box farther away from these things.

Sunshine and great views really help. The most popular location for a cat bed is in front of windows. Not only is this the warmest spot (as long as the window isn't drafty); it also gives him a chance to watch for intruders or birds.

Bad Locations for Cats to Sleep

▶ Drafty areas   ▶ Garage
▶ Outside, unsupervised   ▶ Near the furnace or water heater or cars
▶ Close to a litter box   ▶ Where she may be stepped on

Some cats even like to sleep amid the racket of a noisy household. Most favor spots where they won't be stepped on. Older cats need beds near or on the floor, away from drafts, and close to necessities such as food and water dishes.

Part 2
Cat Life

73   11 ● Scratching Posts, Exercise, and Play

86   12 ● Diet

100   13 ● Hands-On Experience

104   14 ● Hair and Nails

111   15 ● Doctor, Doctor!

117   16 ● Administering Treatments

121   17 ● Yucky Stuff

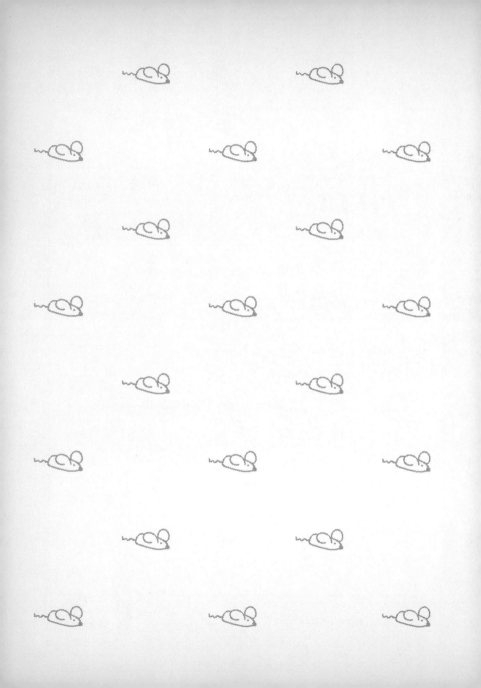

11

Scratching Posts, Exercise, and Play

He seems the incarnation of everything soft and silky and velvety, without a sharp edge in his composition, a dreamer whose philosophy is sleep and let sleep.

Saki

![paw icon] Exercise is as important for cats as it is for people. Although cats sleep a lot, they want to stay in shape for the hunt. Cats pounce, jump, play, chase each other around, and scratch. These activities keep their muscles and reflexes tuned for hunting and pouncing, and also keep their psyches relaxed, confident, and healthy.

All cats can benefit from one or two play times each day. Find a time when you both are in the mood. It's almost always difficult enough to get cats to play, so avoid times when they really don't feel like it. Popular times for my cats are after breakfast and before or after dinner.

Scratching Posts

Scratching is very important exercise. It's natural, which means you don't have to

Shopping List

- ✓ scratching posts and cat trees
- ✓ catnip spray or loose catnip leaves
- ✓ furniture cover (heavy-duty plastic or tablecloth fabric found at fabric stores)
- ✓ upholstery twist pins (found at hardware or fabric stores)
- ✓ cat toys (toys stuffed with catnip; Ping-Pong balls; pipe cleaners; etc.)
- ✓ The Cat Dancer
- ✓ Da Bird by Go Cat

Optional

- ✓ cardboard scratching pad
- ✓ perfume
- ✓ Sticky Paws for Furniture or wide plastic shipping tape or double-stick tape.

See the Products and Resources section in the Appendix for more information.

teach your cat *how* to scratch, only *where* to scratch—on his scratching post or his scratching tree. A cat tree serves the same function as a scratching post, but it's taller and has one or more platforms that the cat can rest on.

Except where explicitly distinguished, when I mention posts and trees, I mean either one.

As a cat owner, you *want* your pet to scratch to strengthen his chest, back, stomach, and shoulders. This releases physical and emotional stress that a cat would otherwise store. A stronger body means more confidence and higher self-esteem, which in turn means fewer behavior problems and lower medical bills. At the same time, as a cat owner, you want to have nice furniture. Training your cat to use a scratching post is the answer.

You will not need a squirt bottle to train your cat to stay off the furniture and use his scratching post. In fact, I can promise you that squirting will *not* yield the results you want. Squirting only stops your cat from scratching in front of you. All it teaches him is to fear squirt bottles; it does not teach him to use his post.

 WARNING ▪ If you're thinking of declawing your cat to avoid scratching problems, beware! See Declawed Cats in the Special Considerations section of this chapter.

Training your cat to use a post is absolutely the easiest lesson to teach. He will understand within a few days. A cat that has been badly trained, abused, or taught incorrectly takes longer, but *will learn*. Your cat is very smart and very eager to show off to you just how well he scratches. In about a month he'll refine his new habit. Kittens, once they are old enough to scratch, learn in just a few days.

Scratching on a good post or climbing a tall cat tree is the best exercise a cat can get, and it's the easiest way for a cat to exercise indoors.

Scratching Post Basics

There is no question that your cat needs a post. Don't expect him to not scratch or to wait to go outside to use a tree. Get a post with a rough surface, such as sisal rope, carpet, or natural bark. Smooth surfaces don't let a cat lock his claws and pull; he needs something rugged.

The scratching post must be sturdy and must not fall, slide, or wiggle while he's using it. The post also should be tall enough—twenty-eight inches or more—to allow your cat to stretch his body full out while standing on his hind legs. It's a good idea to have a few scratching posts and at least one tall cat tree so that no matter where he is in your house, there's a good place to scratch nearby.

true story

Right before I take Louie on his walk, I say, "Here, Louie! Time to go outside!" He runs to the door and waits to have his collar put on. Then I say, "It's time to scratch." He walks over to his post and scratches. If he doesn't scratch, I say, "I can wait longer than you!" And if Louie just pretends to scratch, I say, "What was that? I think you'd better scratch!" It never fails. He turns to his post because he knows that's what earns him outside walks.

Do not place the posts behind furniture or other obstacles. Two good places are near the door where you come in and near the door he uses to go outside. Whenever you see him use the post, praise and reward him. To let your cat know the post is his, spray it with catnip. Occasionally, I'll dab my perfume on things that I really want the cat to know are off-limits. Some cats hate perfume.

Scratching Post Training

If you're training an adult cat, cover vulnerable furniture with heavy plastic or slippery durable fabric such as that used for wipe-clean tablecloths. That way, he'll have no alternative but to use the post, and you'll be able to avoid reprimands while he's in training.

Clean any previously damaged areas to remove scent before covering. Be sure to secure the bottom edge of the protective cover or the cat will reach up under it to scratch. Upholstery twist pins work well for this purpose.

If you have too much furniture to cover, consider confining the cat during those times when you can't watch him, until his training is complete. Make him use his post before he's allowed to leave the confinement room for brief periods. At the same time, place as much protection as you can on the roughest sofas you may own. Confinement shouldn't be necessary for more than a few weeks, because a cat will do practically anything to be free. Scratching is one of the first things he'll do when he's frustrated.

Kittens learn very quickly if you confine them when you can't watch them. (See the information about kittens in the Special Considerations section of this chapter. Also see Chapter 4 for more about confinement.)

 Helpful Hint ▮ If your cat has been taught not to scratch, you need to get him to scratch in front of you. To help retrain a cat, use a *new* lure toy on his *new* scratching post. Also, hide the squirt bottles if you were using them.

To start training, move the post to a high-traffic area and scratch the post yourself for a few seconds while your cat is watching. It might sound silly, but smile and make eye contact with the cat during this period—many cats take their emotional cues from you. Associate happiness with his post. If he uses it, even if just for a split second, praise and pet him lavishly. If he doesn't use it now, be patient.

Cats usually scratch after waking up or eating. As soon as he makes a move to scratch, gently direct or carry him to his post. Speak gently and positively whenever he is near the post. Say his name and pet him if he uses it.

Scratching Posts		
Types	*Descriptions/Comments*	*Source, Approximate Cost*
Cat Posts	Very effective in working the upper body. Sizes and styles vary; the taller, the better. Some are covered with carpet, others with sisal rope, fabric, bark, or another textured material. The twenty-eight-inch sisal-covered Large Katnip Tree from Felix is excellent for enticing cats to scratch. The scratching part is replaceable. (I highly recommend the Felix Katnip Trees. These are my cats' favorite scratching posts. I bought two of them ten years ago and they still look brand new!)	Pet stores, department stores, mail order. The Felix Katnip Post is about $50 plus shipping and handling.
Cat Trees	Cat trees are tall scratching posts, usually with pedestals for the cat to rest. The height helps build both upper and lower body. Carpet-covered models shred but can be re-covered. The Felix Climber extends to the ceiling and is compact for apartments. The parts are replaceable.	Pet stores, mail order. Good ones cost $100 to $300, but they last several years. Yard sale prices range from $1 to $5. The Felix Climber is about $150.
Tree Limb	Get a long tree limb four to six inches thick, with rough bark. It's effective and inexpensive. Secure it in an upright or slanted position by leaning it against something solid. The log can also simply be placed on the floor for horizontal scratching.	Usually free when the city does spring cleanup on trees.
Others	Scratch pads often are made out of corrugated cardboard strips. These pads lie loose on the ground and accommodate a cat that is inclined to scratch the floor. These should complement scratching posts, not replace them. A cat still needs to scratch tall, upright posts. Wall-mountable scratch pads with replaceable pads are available too. Pads that move, such as those that can be hung on doorknobs, generally are not used by cats.	Pet stores, mail order. Prices for cardboard scratch pads range from $4 to $40. Or make your own out of an old cardboard box. Trader Joes carries a very inexpensive cardboard scratch pad.

(See Products and Resources in the Appendix for all products mentioned in the table.)

A cat likes to scratch when he is frustrated and nervous. Use these moments to redirect the cat's energy to the post. Sound proud and encouraging when he turns his anger to his post. He soon will forget that he was angry.

Best Times to Direct Your Cat to His Post

▶ Early morning, right after he wakes up

▶ When you get home from work (many cats love to "show off" when they haven't seen their owners all day)

▶ Before he wants breakfast, lunch, or dinner

▶ After his nap

▶ After eating

▶ Before he wants to go out

▶ Right before scheduled play time

▶ After he uses the litter box

▶ When he's angry, frustrated, happy, or proud

You also can make a game out of it. Wiggle a pipe cleaner or toy up the scratching post so that the cat can't help but claw at it. Play with his lure toy on it. (See the Lure Toys section later in this chapter.) As soon as a claw touches the post, say "Good boy," and pet him. Reinforce this positive association by continuing to play with him on or near the post.

Use food to encourage his good behavior. At feeding time, scratch the post and say "Time to scratch." Then wait. If he doesn't take the hint, hold him so his front legs are extended and he has to grasp the post to keep himself from falling. As soon as one claw becomes caught on the post, praise him and let him go. Reward him with a treat or a wet meal. But taper off the use of food as a reward after the cat has had a few days on the post. Gradually switch to rewarding him with petting, praise, and play.

Your cat will make the connection to using his post even faster when he wants to go outside. A cat that is used to going outside will turn to scratching when he doesn't get his way. Make this behavior a part of his training by keeping a post near the door. Then, before you let him out, make sure he uses the post first. Either wait for him to scratch it or pick him up and make him scratch it by sliding him down his post until a claw catches. After a few days of this, wait for him to scratch the post on his own. Don't let him outside until he does.

WARNING ■ Be careful with your hands around your cat when he is in his tree. He may act a little feisty there, and that's okay. A cat should be allowed to be aggressive on his tree. If you accidentally get scratched while he's on his cat tree, say "Ouch" and walk away. Later, when the cat is away from his tree, check to see if his nails need trimming.

Once your cat begins scratching on his own, it's crucial that you continue to praise and/or pet him for using it every day. He'll especially want to show off when you come home from work.

Don't Scratch That!

The final phase is teaching your cat not to scratch the furniture. Once he's using the post on his own for a month or so, it's time to unveil a piece of furniture. Do it on a day when you will be home, such as when you're doing housework. Keep an eye out. If your cat starts to scratch the furniture, immediately say "No" in a firm yet caring manner. Then gently carry him to the post. As soon as he's at the post, say "Time to scratch" in a sweet, gentle tone. Slide his body down the post until his claws engage. As soon as a claw catches in the post, say "Good boy," release him, and then pet him for a second or two.

Re-cover the piece of furniture when you won't be there, and repeat the process one or more times a day. As the cat becomes more dependable in using the post on his own, gradually remove more of the furniture covers. If the cat has a special spot he likes to scratch, cover it with Sticky Paws (see Products and Resources in the Appendix) or with wide shipping tape or double-stick tape until you are sure he'll behave. Make sure the tape won't damage the furniture before you use it.

If he continues to scratch the sofa after a few weeks, reprimand him more sharply as each occurrence happens. Start showing anger in your voice. Try to get your hands on him as soon as he scratches, and then point him to the sofa and say "No!" again. Then, either carry him to his scratching post or trim a nail while he's in front of the sofa. Either way, as soon as he's near his post or as soon as you have a paw in your hand ready to clip, change to a sweet tone and tell him he's a good boy.

Your cat will learn that the post is the only acceptable place for him to scratch. Once trained, cats seldom make mistakes. Continue to praise him daily and keep his nails trimmed regularly. In the event he does make a mistake, a blunt claw can do little to no damage.

The Great Outdoors

There are many ways to increase your cat's physical activity. Sometimes a cat needs motivation to get enough exercise. To a cat, the outdoors is one of the best motivators around. Nothing arouses his curiosity or his hunting instincts as much. A few cats don't want to go outside, but most cats enjoy it. Consult Chapter 19 for advice about how to train your cat to stay in the yard.

Other Cats

Some cats will play with you when other cats are around, but with some shy cats you need to keep other cats away. Most cats love to play with each other. They'll run, tug, and pull each other, which helps build muscles and confidence. Hang an old sheet over a chair and watch two cats play and dive together. Or give them something as simple as a cardboard box or brown paper bag and watch how they amuse themselves with it.

Lure Toys

Playing with your cat provides additional exercise and helps him build trust and confidence in you. The easiest play motivator is a lure toy. A lure toy is a rod with a thick string or wire that dangles from the end. You can buy lure toys, or you can make them at home quickly and cheaply. Buy a three-foot-long one-quarter-inch wooden dowel or a yardstick from a hardware or crafts store. Or use an old fishing rod. Attach a piece of cord to the end (use tape or tie it on). That's all you need. You also can tie feathers or strips of fabric to the end of the cord.

Mister Lincoln's favorite lure is a Cat Dancer attached to a wire at the end of the rod. This toy has some cardboard strips on the end of a curved springy wire, and is readily available at pet stores, shelters, and through mail-order catalogs.

Another exceptional toy is Da Bird by Go Cat. The fiberglass rod comes with a lifetime guarantee and is light and easy to hold. The lures are replaceable, and come in mylar strips as well as feathers. The lures flutter when moved through the air, and they almost sound like a bird flying, which really gets your cat's attention. (See Products and Resources in the Appendix for more information about both of these toys.)

 Helpful Hint ■ Restrict playing with your cat to one room so he won't annoy you by wanting to play in other rooms where you work, cook, or eat.

Pique your cat's curiosity by keeping the toy out of reach and mysterious. After he's chased it for a few minutes, allow him to grab it. Don't make the toy too easy to catch or he will lose interest.

It's easy to get distracted, so it's better not to talk on the phone or watch TV while you're playing with the cat. Radios are okay, because the constant chatter or sounds cover up smaller sounds that may distract him from playing. Some cats will think that you are talking to them while you're on the phone.

true story

Mister Lincoln will stop playing if I move away from carpet. He will not play on a hard floor.

Tell your cat how wonderful he is when he catches the lure or does a good jump. Encourage him even if he isn't spectacular, and say his name softly, with pride. To help him feel like a proud hunter, allow him to catch the toy often. If he touches it while it's in flight, let it fall down as if he caught it. Let him spend time with his prize before you whisk it away. Give your cat the advantage; let the lure toy be vulnerable prey.

Pretend you're fishing, and "cast" the lure to various spots in the room. It takes a few casts for cats, just like fish, to take the bait. Stop the action every once in a while to give him time to pounce.

Pay attention to which movements your cat likes. Does he like the lure moving high? Low? Fast, slow? In corners? Out in the open? Close or far? Try many variations and see what works. Cats get fascinated when you drag the toy around a corner and keep it there just out of sight. Sometimes it takes patience to get a cat to attack the lure. Many aren't willing to start playing until they've understood the lure's movements, so don't give up too soon.

End the play time when he's lost interest for a while, not when he's having fun. If you must end the play before he's ready to quit, be sure to pet, massage, and cuddle him a little before leaving. Always put the lure toys away so that he can't get at them when you're not there.

Other Toys

Reflect a spot of sunlight off your watch onto the wall or floor, or use a flashlight to encourage your cat to chase. You also can try a laser light pointer, which you can find at pet stores or office supply stores. (This is Louie's favorite. He'll chase the beam all over the place and talk to it, too.) Warning: Be sure never to shine a laser light in his eyes.

Catnip soap bubbles are available from pet stores or catalogs. You also can squirt some catnip spray into a regular bottle of bubble solution.

Ping-Pong balls, paper bags, fake mice, toys stuffed with catnip—anything that can be batted around and pounced on—can attract your cat. Cut off elastic cords, strings, tails, glued-on eyes, yarn, or anything else he could chew off and swallow.

Do *Not* Use These Toys

▶ Balls of string or yarn: Cats can swallow and choke on them. Anything with loose string should be stored away when you're not there.

▶ Toys with decorations glued on: Cut off all decorations before you give the toy to your cat. He could swallow them.

▶ Toys attached to thin elastic—cut off the elastic before giving the toy to your cat.

Spray catnip scent on toys about once a year so he'll be reminded of the things he owns. To maintain the cat's interest in the toys, rotate them through various rooms or hide them for a while every few months.

Special Considerations

Cats, like people, require special considerations regarding exercise. When people are very old or very young we aren't expected to do as much exercise as healthy adults. And disabled people missing fingers, toes, and limbs are prescribed physical therapy and medications to help compensate for their loss and to manage the pain. The same applies to older cats, kittens, and declawed cats.

 WARNING ▥ Never use your hands to play with a cat. You could get hurt. Use a toy.

Older Cats

It's sometimes difficult to get an older cat interested in lure toys. To make it easier for him to get his exercise, provide a scratching post near his bed. Although most older cats won't wander far from home, monitor your older cat closely when he's outside, because he won't be able to protect himself as well as he once could.

Declawed Cats

A declawed cat is handicapped. Don't try to train a declawed cat to use a post. He cannot use a scratching post as a clawed cat would, and he should not be expected to. He won't be able to grasp or dig into the post and may end up frustrated. And he'll fall off carpeted cat trees more often than will a clawed cat. He'll need to exercise some other way.

Lure toys and running around indoors can provide some exercise. Just don't expect too much, because cats aren't inclined to run, and you don't want to "make" a declawed cat run around. It's cruel to force a cat with sore feet to run around or walk a long distance for bathroom, food, or water. We don't expect a loved one who is missing all her toes to park her car in the furthest parking spot. It's not in a cat's nature to run, let alone on compromised, painful feet.

Playing with another cat is good. It's okay if his buddy has claws; other cats recognize handicaps. Supervise him on outside walks where he can climb chainlink fences or rough-barked trees. Remember that he's very clumsy and vulnerable, so you have to watch him. A declawed cat needs constant adult supervision when outside because he cannot properly defend himself.

If possible, teach him to swim. Teach him in a children's or chemical-free portable pool, or in a deep bathtub or shallow lake. Start with very short lessons, holding the cat in place while he moves his arms and legs. Be careful not to get water in his mouth, nose, or ears. Keep the experience positive by having his favorite treat and a dry towel waiting for him when he gets out of the pool. Gradually increase the time and his freedom as his tolerance and interest increase.

true story

I try to take the time to play with my cats every day. They really look forward to it. Louie leaps and bounds up the stairs toward the playroom to let me know it's time to play! We spend about twenty minutes having fun with their lure toys.

Kittens

Teaching a kitten where to scratch is very easy. Whenever you want to let him out of his confinement room, take him to the post first. Hold his paws up to it. Once one claw catches, reward him immediately by petting. Let him scratch more if he wants to, and then carry him out of the confinement room. The sooner you start noticing a kitten actively scratching his post, all on his own, the sooner you can give him access to the rest of the house. Some kittens may understand when they're as young as five months.

As long as there are cat posts available and you are there to say "Good boy," he'll use them several times a day—until he gets very, very old.

Diet

When clients say their cat won't listen or has a behavior problem, my first question usually is, "What does he eat?" Nutrition directly affects a cat's ability to listen, to behave well, and to be healthy. A healthful diet is part of the long-term solution for any behavior problem.

Diet and Behavior

In 1932, Dr. Francis Pottenger began a ten-year study on cats. Though its purpose was related to dentistry, it has become well known for what it revealed about the effects of diet on cat behavior. In the study, cats that were fed only raw food remained healthier and developed fewer behavioral problems than did cats that were fed cooked food. For this reason it is believed by some that a raw food diet is best for your cat.

Shopping List—Cat Food

Choose from brands like these:

✔ Active Life Cat Food, AvoDerm, Advanced Pet Diets, California Natural, Felidae, Flint River Ranch, Innova, Matrix, Merrick, One Earth, Petguard, Pinnacle, Prairie, Precise, Spot's Stew, Wysong. (These foods are naturally preserved.) Avoid cheap brands.

✔ Anitra's Vita-Mineral Mix, Wysong's food supplements, and other food supplements

See the Products and Resources section in the Appendix for more information.

Unfortunately, it is not convenient to feed your cat raw food. Although you can make up big batches and freeze homemade raw food, it takes time and energy that a lot of us don't have. Pet food companies nowadays sell frozen raw pet foods. Bagged in small portions, you simply take one serving out of the freezer and let it thaw. (See the section on Raw Food later in this chapter for companies that sell frozen raw pet food products.) Cooked homemade food can be frozen too.

Another important consideration is that commercially available dry cat food is hard on the kidneys. Many people think that a dry-food-only diet leads to kidney problems, which are a common cause of death for house cats.

 Cats Are Like People ▦ Neither people nor cats can tolerate the same food every day. Eventually, we will have poor manners and poor health, become finicky, and make our kidneys work harder.

I recommend a combination of wet and dry foods along with some dietary supplements. Feed your cat a variety of brands and flavors to help ensure a more balanced diet. No single food can have everything a cat needs.

Dry food and canned food should have meat as the primary ingredient. Cats are carnivores and must eat meat to stay healthy. Read the label on every can and every bag. Chicken, chicken meal, or some other meat should be the first ingredient. Many experts recommend that two of the first four ingredients should be meat.

Buy high-quality cat foods. These typically don't have ingredients that may cause health problems that could result in higher medical bills. To find high-quality foods, look in pet stores and health food stores. Ingredients in many grocery store discount brands aren't as good. Cheaper brands can contain what is known as "4-D meat": dead, down, dying, or diseased meats, which can include cancerous tumors, not to mention dogs and cats, fur, tags, and flea collars may get tossed in the rendering pit and ground into pet food. Cats should not eat dog food. It doesn't have enough protein. Buy cat food.

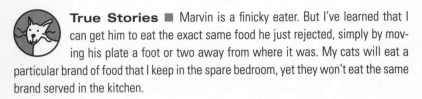 **True Stories** ■ Marvin is a finicky eater. But I've learned that I can get him to eat the exact same food he just rejected, simply by moving his plate a foot or two away from where it was. My cats will eat a particular brand of food that I keep in the spare bedroom, yet they won't eat the same brand served in the kitchen.

Wet Food

When I refer to wet food I'm talking about canned cat food, homemade food, and table scraps. These should be the main part of a cat's diet. As mentioned before, dry food can lead to kidney problems.

Unless instructed otherwise by your veterinarian, feed two or three small wet meals a day. As little as a teaspoon per meal will satisfy some cats. Feed smaller and more frequent meals to kittens, or to cats who are weak, old, or nursing babies.

Bring refrigerated food to room temperature before serving it—cats don't like cold food. After half an hour, refrigerate leftover canned cat food in a glass container to prevent lead from leaching from the can.

 Wet Food Servings? ■ Give him a trial serving and see how much he eats in five to ten minutes. If he doesn't finish it, give him less next time. If he eats it all, try a little more next time.

Give your cat meat table scraps, homemade cat food (see the next section), and raw meats and vegetables. Feed a wide variety of canned foods. This helps give him a wide variety of food sources.

It's hard to find canned food without at least some fish ingredient, but you should avoid canned food that is primarily fish. Too much canned fish in the diet can make your cat lethargic and can even cause illness.

Canned tuna is addictive to cats and will deplete vitamin E. Lack of vitamin E can lead to fatigue and stress, and some cats might start over-grooming. I avoid feeding my cats canned tuna, but I do give them some fresh raw tuna about twice a month for a treat.

 When to Feed Wet Meals ▬ Feed wet meals around your work schedule. Try to feed at the same times each day so your cats have something to look forward to.

Don't buy canned food containing sodium nitrate or sodium nitrite, because they are suspected carcinogens. They often are used in cured meats such as hot dogs and sausages and in canned pet foods.

 When buying cat food, look for:
▶ Canned cat foods that are labeled "natural"
▶ Dry foods preserved with vitamin E (tocopherols) or vitamin C (ascorbic acid)

Homemade Food

Tasty homemade food can be a special and healthful treat for your cat. What's more, with homemade foods, you can control the quality. Homemade food is superior to store-bought food.

I know it's hard enough just to have time to cook for your own family. Here are some simple recipes to get you started. (See Products and Resources in the Appendix for recipe books.)

Chop all cooked meats and raw vegetables as small as peas, or use a food processor. The more organic ingredients you can use, the better.

Quick Dinner

½ cup meat (cut-up cooked lamb, poultry, rabbit, fish, or raw ground beef)
2 tablespoons cooked brown rice, quinoa, or couscous
1 jar of vegetable baby food (peas, broccoli, etc.)

Stir together. Serve at room temperature. Serves two or three cats.

Louie's Favorite Lunch

You can substitute ingredients to add variety to this recipe. Broccoli and carrots are good sources of vitamins A, C, and D as well as calcium.

2 tablespoons olive oil or butter (not margarine!)
1 carrot, finely grated
½ cup green vegetable, finely grated (broccoli, green pepper, parsley, etc.)
1 pound raw meat (poultry, beef, buffalo, lamb, rabbit, or boneless fish)
1 can (about 2 cups) low-sodium chicken broth or bouillon
1 cup cooked brown rice, cooked quinoa, or Sojourner Farms European-
    Style Pet Food Mix (see Products and Resources in the Appendix)
2 teaspoons dietary supplement (see Supplements section of this chapter)

Heat oil or butter over medium-high heat. Brown the meat. Add broth and vegetables. If using poultry or rabbit, reduce the heat and simmer until done; the other meats won't need to be cooked any longer. Remove from heat, add grain, and stir. Serve warm but not hot. Store the rest in the refrigerator or freeze in small portions. Makes 20 quarter-cup servings.

WARNING ▨ Cats with medical conditions or behavior problems may not be able to eat certain foods. Tailor any of the suggested food, recipes, or menus to your cat's condition, and follow the veterinarian's advice.

Beef Jerky

I included this recipe because it always draws a crowd—or should I say, a clowder. (The actual name for a group of cats is "clowder.") You will need a food dehydrator for this.

1 pound very thinly sliced beef
¼ cup low-sodium tamari or soy sauce
1 teaspoon liquid smoke
1 tablespoon 100 percent pure maple syrup
½ teaspoon dietary supplement (see Supplements later in this chapter)

Mix liquids together and stir into beef. Let set for 15 minutes. Spread the mixture on the dehydrator pan. Dry in food dehydrator one to two days. When the jerky is completely dry, break it into small bits. Makes about 9 ounces of jerky.

Cat Treats

The more organically grown/hormone-free ingredients you can use, the better:

- Steamed spinach, squash or kale with butter
- Baked potato with butter
- Raw egg yolk (not raw egg white)
- Coconut milk
- Plain yogurt
- Cooked turkey, chicken, lamb, roast beef, buffalo, or rabbit (cut the meat into small bits and store in freezer in plastic bags
- Leftover cooked meat cut into small bits
- Roasted chicken necks (including bone, crumbled into sections)
- Raw ground beef or buffalo
- ½ teaspoon baby food with meat (no onion powder)
- Restaurant leftovers (no sugar)
- Buttered popcorn

- Smoked oysters packed in olive oil
- Avocado
- Cheese (cottage cheese, parmesan, cheddar, Swiss, etc.)
- Oatmeal with cream
- Pancakes with butter
- Stuffed cabbage

Dry Food

As mentioned earlier, a cat's diet should be wet food. If you are feeding some dry food, feed a variety. Do not feed just one brand; set out three different brands in three different bowls. Buy small bags and when one is empty, open a different brand.

If your cat is sick, overweight, has a litter box problem, or you worry about roaches, keep the dry-food bowls covered. Unless otherwise instructed by your veterinarian, uncover the bowls for about twenty minutes twice a day, so your cat can eat some of the dry food in addition to the wet meals he is getting.

Contrary to popular belief, eating dry food does not alleviate dental problems.

Preservatives

Some experts believe that several of the common ingredients used for preserving dry foods are dangerous. Look for food preserved with tocopherols (vitamin E) or ascorbic acid (vitamin C), which are natural and nutritious preservatives.

Avoid dry food that contains these ingredients:

- **Ethoxyquin.** Originally designed as a rubber hardener, pesticide, and herbicide, this chemical is suspected of causing liver disease, kidney disease, skin problems, birth defects, and vitamin E deficiencies. Pet-food makers often use it because it's inexpensive.

- **BHA, BHT.** These common preservatives are suspected of causing liver and kidney damage, immune deficiencies, and behavior problems. In England, BHA and BHT are banned for consumption by children, but in the United States both preservatives are used in food made for human consumption as well as in pet foods.

- **Propyl gallate.** This is another preservative commonly used in the United States but banned in England. It is suspected of causing the same health problems as BHA and BHT.

Raw Food

You may not have time to prepare regular homemade raw food meals every day, but try to use them as frequently as possible. They provide nutrients that are missing from cooked foods.

You can find recipes and instructions for raw food meals in *The New Natural Cat* and *Reigning Cats and Dogs* (see Products and Resources in the Appendix).

Raw food diet sources:
www.bravorawdiet.com
www.amorepetfoods.com
www.naturesvariety.com

Many raw pet food products are available frozen in one-serving portions.

 Homemade food is great. ■ A food processor will speed up the preparation, but simply cutting up the food is fine, too. Try any of these, alone or in combination:
- ▶ fresh organic meats and vegetables
- ▶ whole organic grains (such as cooked brown rice, quinoa)
- ▶ table scraps

  Grains to add to raw or cooked meats: Sojourner Farms European-Style Pet Food Mix, Urban King, Forage Formula

Feeding Kittens

Wet meals are especially important to kittens. Feed kittens five small wet meals a day, more if you have time. Pay careful attention to the ingredients of all foods, because a kitten's small body is ultrasensitive. Specially formulated "kitten" foods are okay, but not required.

Supplements

Food supplements help replace nutrients that are destroyed by cooking or are otherwise not present. Supplements by Wysong and Anitra's Vita-Mineral Mix are designed to help bridge the gap between raw and cooked food. See Products and Resources in the Appendix for more information. These supplements can be added to wet or dry foods. It's also good to periodically switch brands of supplements as well as food, so that your cat benefits from a variety of nutrients.

Feeding Tips

Because some cats cannot eat amidst noise and commotion, create a quiet, peaceful atmosphere when feeding your cat. You might need to serve food away from where your dog eats.

Establish a schedule for feedings. Developing a routine is as important for cats as it is for people. Knowing when he's to be fed gives your cat a sense of security and belonging. You might want to structure cat mealtimes around household meals so that the cat feels included and part of the atmosphere. Don't feed your cat as soon as you get out of bed. Wait until you've showered, made tea, and gotten the newspaper. You don't want him waking you up every morning to be fed.

Call your cat with same phrase every mealtime, like "Here, Louie." This helps train him to come when called. Don't feed a cat when he is whining or begging unless it's really time for him to eat. Wait until your cat is quiet and respectful before placing any food in front of him.

Use a clean glass or ceramic food bowl that is wide enough for his whiskers. Don't use aluminum or plastic bowls. Aluminum can get into the food; plastic bowls harbor bacteria and could contribute to what is known as "feline acne."

If your cat vomits after eating or is eating too fast, spread out his food on a plate to slow him down.

Water

Cats who regularly eat wet food drink very little water. Cats on raw food diets may only drink once every one or two days. Set out glass or ceramic bowls of clean water. Be sure to change the water daily and wash the bowls occasionally because dust will collect in the bottom.

Cats can be very sensitive to chlorine; if you have chlorinated tap water, let the water sit for twenty-four hours so that much of the chlorine can escape. Chlorine is toxic and can cause cancer and health problems in humans. Tap water has made some cats sick with diarrhea or other unexplained symptoms. Using filtered or bottled water will eliminate the wait because the chlorine has already been removed (given that the filter is designed to remove chlorine).

WARNING ■ If your cat drinks water constantly, he could have a serious medical condition. See the veterinarian immediately; get a full exam and have the cat's urine checked. If the cat is older, have his blood checked as well, to make sure his kidneys are functioning properly.

It's best not to let your cat drink out of the toilet bowl. Water in the toilet is not always safe to drink. Also, the seat could fall on him and hurt him.

Catnip

Catnip is an herb you can grow indoors or out, or buy from a pet store. Most cats love it. Catnip helps relieve stress and boredom and helps provide some fiber in your cat's diet. Contrary to myth, catnip is not addictive to cats. They won't sell their blood or prostitute themselves to get catnip. You may, however, have a cat that can pull the catnip jar out of a cupboard and open it (as my Moses used to do). Keep catnip leaves in a sealed container in the refrigerator or freezer. This also helps to keep it fresh.

Use loose leaves for your cat to eat and roll in; apply catnip spray to toys. Buy only *organic* leaves to avoid harmful herbicides and pesticides.

Treat your cats to catnip once or twice a week. Declawed cats, spraying cats, or cats with litter box problems could use more. Put catnip leaves on a piece of heavy fabric or newspaper. Leave it out for half an hour or so. Roll up the fabric and store it away. Next time, add a little fresh catnip to the pile.

Sometimes a cat will become a little feisty when smelling or eating catnip. He's being protective of it, so don't touch him. He may play too rough with you while he's feeling like a "real cat." He could get feisty with other cats too, but that's okay (that's their job).

Spray catnip on your cat's toys, beds, and scratching posts about once a year to tell him what's his and what isn't.

Eating Problems

Cats are notorious for being fussy eaters. Cat owners often throw away or give away cat food because their cat "just won't eat it!" Ask your pet store what their return policy is on cat food. You might be very surprised: Many pet food stores guarantee your cat will like it or you'll get your money back. Ask your pet store if they have food samples.

This chapter recommends feeding a wide variety of foods to your cat. However, change in diet can have the same affect on a cat as when we humans improve our diet. Your cat may lose weight or experience changes in stools and moods. Have sympathy on your cat if you're weaning him off of his regular food. It is like us quitting chocolate, coffee, bread, or sugar—we tend to feel worse and act worse before we feel better.

Changing Diets

If the cat is older, and you are switching him to a higher-quality diet, make gradual changes over a two-week period. Young, healthy cats often can be abruptly switched to better foods. A cat may experience moodiness when switched from a relatively poor diet to a more healthful one. He also may get diarrhea. If a kitten gets diarrhea, take him to the veterinarian. If an adult has diarrhea more than two days in a row, see the veterinarian.

Keep to a Minimum

▶ Canned food containing sodium nitrates or nitrites
▶ Cheap brands
▶ Artificial preservatives

Mr. Finicky

For any finicky eater, make sure the cat is not sick. Many old cats will appear to be finicky eaters, but really are beginning to die. It's not uncommon for the cat to be dead within a week or so after the owner realizes he's not just being finicky.

Call the veterinarian when:

- An old cat misses eating one day.
- An adult cat misses two days.
- A kitten (after being weaned) misses one meal; kittens are always hungry.

After eating the same food day after day, cats may at first refuse to eat anything else. Your cat may even go on a mini hunger strike to see if you will produce the food he's addicted to. Don't give in if you're certain your cat is just being finicky! Try these tactics instead:

- Sit down and stay with him while he eats. He might need you to be there with him, especially if he's new in your household.
- To stimulate his appetite, massage or play with him before feeding. Massaging your cat and playing with him does wonders to work up an appetite!

If he doesn't want to eat wet food, try these tips:

- Use a saucer instead of a bowl. Use a clean one every day.
- Move his plate away from the other cats.
- Feed him a bit of food from your finger. Or try a little baby food, and gradually change to homemade or canned food.
- Tempt him with home-cooked chicken, lamb, turkey, buffalo, or beef as treats.
- Buy small cans of food. Some cats like their food fresh out of the can and won't eat leftovers.

Special Considerations

Many cat owners think their cat needs low-fat foods if he's overweight, older, or less active. And maybe that works for some cats. In my experience with both cats and people, I have found that cats and people who consume "low-cal" diets are often the ones with weight problems.

Diets for Obese or Senior Cats

The best weight-reduction program for a cat is a high-quality, balanced diet. Foods labeled "less active" or "lite" often just make the cat want to eat more. With premium cat food and homemade food, cats will usually stabilize at a healthy weight.

Limit feeding dry food to no more than once or twice a day. If the advice in this chapter doesn't help, consult the diet books referenced in the Products and Resources section of the Appendix.

Senior cats can benefit by eating mostly wet food, small meals, several times a day. Add a little water to each wet meal to help flush his aging kidneys. Older cats can get by with less fat than younger cats, but they still need high-quality protein.

Foods to Avoid

- Chocolate: it's poisonous to cats
- Sugar: depletes the immune system
- Artificial sweeteners
- MSG (monosodium glutamate)
- White flour
- Raw egg white: depletes vitamin E
- Canned tuna
- Onion powder: can cause anemia; check ingredient lists of baby foods
- Pork: can contain parasites
- Milk: can cause diarrhea; raw organic milk is okay
- Hydrogenated fats
- Hot dogs
- Cake, cookies
- Dog food

Hands-On Experience

Touch is one of the most powerful tools you have to prolong the health and well-being of your cat. Your hands can heal, soothe, teach trust, and stimulate appetite. But if you try to handle a cat at the wrong time or in the wrong way, you could get hurt. This chapter talks about how to hold, pet, and massage a cat in ways that can benefit both cat and owner.

How to Pick Up, Hold, and Let Go of a Cat

Pay attention to your cat's likes and dislikes. A cat may not like being picked up, but doesn't mind being held. Or there may be certain times of each day when he may not like to be touched, yet at other times he will. Never handle an angry cat; you could get hurt.

Approach your cat slowly. Let him sniff you. Spend a second or two petting him. Then, very gently and slowly, pick him up.

Once he's in your arms, speak softly and gently say his name. While he's in your arms, give support to both the front of the body and the hindquarters. Cradle him so that he doesn't feel confined. Cats usually like to stay upright in your arms, though a few will lie on their backs.

Let him go when he wants to leave. Be very gentle. Let him down slowly. Never hold a cat against his will. As soon as he shows signs of being fussy, wait until he's calmed for a second or two, then let him go. Don't keep holding on to him until he gets too antsy to hold. If your cat knows that he can get away at will, he'll be more comfortable the next time he's held.

Do not hold a cat when he's likely to be suddenly frightened, such as when he's meeting a new cat or dog or walking near an appliance that makes noise. A suddenly frightened cat can accidentally hurt you while he's trying to get away or is overwhelmed with fear.

 WARNING ■ Never handle an angry cat. You could get hurt.

If you have to pick him up when he doesn't want to be, don't call him. Go to him instead.

Touch Techniques

Start with short sessions to build up his trust in you. Gradually increase the time you pet or massage him.

Petting

Cats love being scratched and rubbed under the chin, on the face, on top of the head—places they can't lick themselves. And you can find special places, too, maybe his shoulders or at the base of his tail. Besides scratching and petting with your fingers, try full, open hands with purposeful strokes, like the way cat moms use their tongues to caress their young.

Massage

Massage is a potent relaxant and pain reliever. Massage is basically some serious petting for the whole body. Muscular cats tend to prefer deep massage, while kittens, old, or declawed cats usually prefer a light touch.

Place a towel under your cat during the massage, because a lot of hair usually comes off in the process. Speak softly and use slow, gentle movements. Explore different parts of your cat's body. My cats enjoy having their feet, shoulders, stomach, face, and thighs massaged.

When you touch a cat's foot he may pull it toward his body. Go with it. Let his foot stay wherever he wants it while you massage it. If he gets a little fussy, move back into an area that he likes.

 True Story ■ My cats enjoy having their feet massaged a lot. They spread their toes wide while I rub between each one.

Give him a chance to appreciate your touch but stop before he gets upset or agitated from excessive handling. He may cry first (like Mr. Lincoln does) then bite if he's over-handled. It's good to end with success and with him being good, not agitated. If he's likely to meow before biting you, stop petting when he asks politely (meows). Don't wait until he has to bite you to get your attention that the massage is over. Some cats may like only fifteen-second massages; some may want five minutes. (Louie likes three times that.) When it's time to end the massage, stroke him on his head a few times, gently tell him he's a good boy, and walk away slowly, as if leaving a baby in a crib for his nap.

Special Considerations

Handle kittens as much as possible. Scientific tests have shown that kittens with just twenty minutes of daily handling are more likely to be better companions.

Massage is especially valuable for an only cat, because he gets no grooming or physical contact from another cat.

Declawed cats get an additional benefit from massage. The muscles in their shoulders and forelegs are likely to be sore from compensating for missing toes.

Very gentle, daily massage for sick or elderly cats can help relieve stress and pain. Holding an infirm cat or laying your hands gently on or under him while using soothing words may be enough.

Hair and Nails

When it comes to grooming, cats are pretty good at taking care of themselves. But because he's living indoors, your cat will need some help with grooming. Claws need to be trimmed and hair needs to be brushed. Grooming him once in a while can help keep your home nice and your cat happy. In this chapter, you'll learn how to trim nails and brush your cat without a fuss.

Trimming Claws

If your cat accidentally scratches you or snags your shirt, it's time for a trim. Trimming claws is one of the easiest things you can do to a cat. It can be much faster than cutting your own nails. I recommend nail trimmers made especially for cats. Stainless steel, high-quality models can last many decades.

Before you trim his front claws the first time, work with his front feet without any attempt to trim. Wait until he's in a mood to be touched. Hold him or leave him in his bed while you massage his

Shopping List

✓ brush
✓ comb
✓ shedding blade
✓ towel

Optional

✓ chamois cloth
✓ rounded scissors
✓ electric shears
✓ shampoo

See the Products and Resources section in the Appendix for more information.

body, working your way to his feet. Massage his foot. Rub between his toes. Press on the pads of his feet to make the claws extend, and then release them. If he starts putting up a fuss, let go of his feet. Don't give up too easily, though. Try again the next time you see him napping or relaxing.

After a few days of getting him used to having his feet touched, put the nail trimmer in the palm of your hand before you approach him. Hold his paw in one hand while saying "Good boy." Gently squeeze the pad of the paw so that the claws extend. Talk sweetly to him just as you do when you massage his feet. Cut about half-way between the tip of the claw and the quick (where pink shows through). Begin by trimming only one claw a day. Gradually add more claws. Keep the experience positive by always ending before he gets fussy. Each time, reward him by massaging, petting, playing, or taking him on an outside walk. Eventually, you'll only need to tell him how good he is by petting him for a few seconds after his trim.

true story

My husband says he wishes his nails were as easy to trim as our four cats' claws are.

Once the cat is used to getting trimmed, you'll need to trim all claws about once a month. Be very careful when trimming a claw. Cutting into the quick causes bleeding and is painful. If you hurt your cat while trimming, immediately say you're sorry and comfort him. Quickly trim one more nail and then let him go. Play with him to distract him from what just happened. Try again the next day.

Don't trim his nails on or around his post or cat tree. You don't want him to make an association between the two activities.

If the cat growls, stop trimming, say nothing, and leave the room immediately. On the next day, cut two, or even just one nail. Leave on a friendly note, before he has a chance to growl.

For hind claws, use the same steps as above. Trim hind claws when your cat is sleeping or sitting quietly on your lap. Trim one or two claws at a one sitting. As he gets used to the process, cut more claws. Eventually your cat will learn to love getting his claws trimmed. My cats often purr while I cut their nails—they love the attention! After all, who *doesn't* like their feet pampered?

Even if your cat is declawed, his back claws will need trimming because declawing typically isn't performed on hind feet. Declawed cats tend to bite more, and can be more sensitive about being handled than are clawed cats. You may need to provide food treats to distract your declawed cat during trimming. You also could try to cut a few claws while he's asleep.

Hair

Any cat that has hair will shed. And longhaired cats get matted hair. Professional groomers can help you get rid of shedding hair and prevent matting, but I recommend that you do as much of it yourself as you can. It's a good opportunity for quality time between you and your cat, and it's less stressful if someone he knows works on him.

Did You Know? ■ A frightened cat will lose hair within seconds. It's a safeguard so that when he gets into a fight, he doesn't lose skin, too. When another animal grabs him with claws or teeth, his fur will come out easily and loosen the animal's grip. You may notice that your cat loses a lot more hair at the veterinarian's office than he does at home.

How Often Is Grooming Needed?

A cat's grooming schedule depends on his hair length, the amount of time he spends outside, and whether he's an only cat. Some cats may need brushing once a day; others only need to be brushed once a month. Cats who go outdoors roll in dirt or on concrete, which helps remove loose hair, so they may be able to go longer between grooming sessions. Shorthaired indoor cats may need to be brushed every one or two weeks. Longhaired cats need to be brushed more frequently.

True Story ■ After living in a stranger's garage for two months, a longhaired, declawed Persian cat was rescued by a local shelter. The cat's coat was as heavily matted as a tightly woven carpet, and so thick that you couldn't even poke your finger through to her skin. Except for her head, I couldn't even tell she was a cat. We had to sedate her while two of us worked for ninety minutes to shave all the mats off with electric shears. She turned out to be a gorgeous cat.

Choosing Grooming Tools

- Brushes and combs come in a wide variety of natural and synthetic bristles, wire, plastic, or rubber. The type of brush or comb you use depends on what your cat likes and the type of tool *you* feel works best. My husband thinks the bent wire brushes are more effective at collecting hair; I prefer using a shedding blade.
- Stainless steel pet combs are good for getting tangles out of long hair. Brushes are nice for a lighter touch.
- You can use scissors to cut out clumps of matted hair. Always hold a comb between scissors and skin to prevent accidental cuts. For more safety, use scissors with rounded tips.
- A shedding blade, which is a hoop-shaped strip of metal with a sawtooth edge and an attached handle, is especially good for removing fine hair. Use a damp rag to collect the hair the blade picks up.
- You can dampen a chamois cloth, spread it out on your open hand, and rub it firmly over the cat's coat to remove loose hair. Keep the cat away from drafts until he's dry.

- Some hair can become so matted that a comb and scissors simply won't work. If you brush your cats regularly, you should be able to prevent this. If necessary, you can use electric shears to remove matting close to the skin, but be careful. It's easy to nick him.
- Your fingers are one of the best grooming tools available, especially for shorthaired cats. Remove loose hair by roughing up your cat's coat with your fingertips and then stroking it back down. Use a damp cloth to pick up any loose hair.

Grooming How-To's

- Find a time when your cat is in a loving mood. Put him on your lap, on his bed, or on a counter with a towel underneath him. Pick a space big enough for him to stretch out.
- Rub him in his favorite spot to get him in a good mood. If he starts getting in a bad mood, stop grooming for the day.
- Start with the neck, chin, and head, or wherever his favorite places are. If he tries to get up and walk away, gently push him back down and immediately resume grooming. If he gets up again, let him go.

Cats Are Like People ■ The condition of our coat/skin is a clue to what we're eating and how we are handling stress.

- Start brushing slowly, with the grain. Take short strokes, lengthening them as he relaxes. If you use a shedding blade, start with short, slow, raking motions, moving with the grain, to remove the loose hair. Then try pushing some hair so it leans against the grain. Starting at the base of that area, use the blade to rake the hair back so it lies in its normal direction.
- Once you've gained his trust, try a new area of his body that he's willing to let you brush.

- The legs on shorthaired cats shouldn't need much grooming.
- Keep the grooming pleasurable for him. Be gentle and talk to him while you work.
- Stop the grooming session before he becomes agitated or before you brush him bald (which is easy to do if he really likes to be brushed). Too much grooming can make some cats moody, which is something you need to avoid. Gently massage him again, tell him what a good boy he is, and slowly walk away. Leave him with a positive image about grooming.

Shampooing

Because shampoo removes the natural oils from cat hair, you should bathe your cat as little as possible. Regular brushing prevents the need to shampoo a cat. I only shampoo my cats if they're really dirty or smelly, otherwise about every four years. This may mean that a cat gets shampooed as few as half a dozen times in his entire lifetime. A cat that has body odor all the time may have a serious health problem; see the veterinarian if you have any doubts.

If you do need to shampoo him, be very careful not to get water near his nose. Cats can easily get a cold or upper respiratory infection that way. Shampoo as gently as possible, using very little shampoo. I like shampooing my cats with Earthbath Totally Natural Cat Shampoo (*www.earthbath.com*). It's gentle, safe, natural, and smells nice. Keep the water on a warm, low, gentle flow. A hair dryer startles most cats, so towel-dry him as soon as he's rinsed. Keep him away from all drafts until he's completely dry.

Special Support for Double-Declawed Cats

If your cat has both front and back claws removed:

- Inspect and clean his ears a few times each year. (See the Cleaning Ears section of Chapter 16, Administering Treatments.)

- Brush and groom him frequently. Help him maintain his coat by letting him roll around on a hard, rough surface. Cats like to groom themselves outside in the dirt on a sunny day.
- Scratch his chin and head more often. Rub his face and neck more. Don't massage him in places he doesn't seem to like.
- Install a Kitty Korner Komber Self-Grooming Aid for Cats. This plastic brush attaches to the corner of a wall and can help a double-declawed cat scratch the difficult places. It's found in most pet stores.

Helpful Hints ■ While brushing, inspect your cat's body for abnormalities such as lumps, swelling, or scabs. Report any problems to your veterinarian.

If you have more than one cat, they can groom and play with each other, which helps with both grooming and exercising.

Cats are smarter than
dogs. You can't get
eight cats to pull a
sled through snow.

Jeff Valdez

15

Doctor, Doctor!

🐾 Don't gamble with your cat's health. While it is important to treat cat diseases as soon as you recognize the symptoms, it's best to leave the diagnosis and treatment to a veterinarian. This chapter will help you determine whether your cat may be sick. If you have any doubt about your cat's health, call the veterinarian immediately.

A Healthy Cat

Somehow cats have gotten the reputation of hiding all the time or being constantly skittish. While most cats will run and hide at the first sign of danger, that's simply because they are afraid. As soon as they become secure in their surroundings, they have less reason to be scared. Rather than hiding, cats are much more likely to:

- Play
- Act curious, attentive, alert
- Sniff things, including the air

Shopping list

✔ cat carrier case
✔ towel for carrier
✔ stocking with dried catnip or lavender
✔ cat treats for carrier case and veterinarian's office

See the Products and Resources section in the Appendix for more information.

- Have a good appetite and show interest in food (remember, kittens are always hungry)
- Enjoy being around other cats and people and show interest in family activities
- Use the litter box faithfully
- Groom themselves several times a day
- Walk and jump with balance and coordination
- Scratch the scratching post several times a day
- Occasionally run and pounce on imaginary things

Signs of Illness

Even healthy cats occasionally get sick. There are some common symptoms of illness that warrant immediate attention from the veterinarian.

Call the vet if your cat:

- Urinates outside the litter box
- Has blood in his urine
- Frequently misses meals or exhibits a change in appetite
- Is constantly thirsty
- Shows unprovoked aggression or sudden change in mood
- Acts lethargic or withdrawn
- Has labored or irregular breathing
- Sneezes, wheezes, or coughs
- Has white gums
- Has pus around eyes or nose
- Overgrooms or is losing hair
- Stops grooming
- Trembles, shakes, or seems feverish
- Vomits or has diarrhea (if a kitten); has chronic vomiting or diarrhea (if an adult)
- Frequently cries or whimpers

- Has constant body odor
- Has lumps, swelling, or open sores
- Obsessively scratches at ears
- Licks around the anus (veterinarian can check to see if anal glands are impacted)
- Walks with his head tilted to one side

Finding a Good Veterinarian

Most people hate going to the doctor. Cats aren't any different. The first step toward making veterinarian visits go well is finding a good doctor.

Ask around or look in the yellow pages for veterinarians who describe themselves as "alternative," "holistic," or "old-fashioned." When you call, ask about the vet's position on declawing. Quite often, veterinarians who refuse to declaw are more in tune with and concerned about your cat's needs. This probably will rule out a lot of veterinarians, but don't get discouraged.

Find out whether the vet is knowledgeable about natural or home remedies, not just antibiotics, antidepressants, tranquilizers, or steroids.

Also ask what he or she charges for checkups as well as specific procedures. Prices for the same procedures can vary by more than 100 percent.

When you call a veterinarian you're considering, see how patient and receptive he or she is to your concerns. If the people in the office seem uninterested or authoritarian, find another veterinarian.

Tips for Trips to the Veterinarian

Making the trip to the doctor can be traumatic for cats. For most cats, this is the only time they leave the house. Even if only taken to the veterinarian once a year, the cat will remember the experience. Many hold grudges. But there are ways to lessen the amount of resentment your cat may keep:

- Leave a cat carrier open and accessible in the house to help your cat get used to it being around. Put a towel or pillow in it. This way, your cat will associate the carrier more with taking a nap than with a trip to the doctor.
- If you're going to a twenty-four-hour emergency clinic, call first so they can be prepared.
- Make a list of symptoms you've noticed and questions to ask the veterinarian. Include questions about recommended medications, as well as their cost and potential side effects.
- To make the trip more relaxing, put a stocking filled with dried catnip or dried lavender into his carrier case.
- If he resists, put him in the case, hind end first, as quickly as possible. If he walks into the carrier by himself, praise him for being so good.
- Give him a food treat every time he enters the carrier whether you had to help or not.
- If you are crunched for time and he's refusing to get into the carrier, put a towel over him and shove him (gently!) into the case, leaving the towel with him. As soon as he's in and the door is shut, say "Good boy!" and give him a treat.
- Some veterinarians make house calls. If you have a number of cats, the time and hassle you can save will make up for the extra cost of having the doctor make the trip.

At the Doctor's Office

Once you've been taken to the exam room, let your cat out of his carrier to explore the room. Talk to him sweetly, pet him, and play with him. Give him a treat.

Stay with your cat unless the veterinarian strictly forbids your presence, or your cat is putting up a fight. Keep in mind that veterinarians often don't want you in the room when drawing blood, inserting microchips or during other procedures where they must be quick, yet firm, in handling your cat. Your being in the room makes your cat feel safer and it also helps you to have an understanding of what the veterinarian is doing for your cat.

Tell the veterinarian about concerns you might have regarding the cat's eating, drinking, and litter box habits. Also mention whether your cat is having trouble walking or breathing, or has stopped grooming himself.

While your cat is being examined, talk to him and comfort him. Tell him he's being good. In the meantime, watch as the veterinarian checks the cat's ears, teeth, and respiratory and heart rhythms.

Don't allow the use of an injected anesthesia for routine procedures such as ear or dental cleanings or drawing blood. If sedation is really necessary, ask your veterinarian for safer alternatives to injections. Many people have told me that their dog or cat never woke up from a "routine teeth cleaning."

true story

A few days after Louie was neutered he developed an infection. His temperature went to 107 degrees and he stopped eating. We took him back to the veterinarian, who had to operate again. When Louie was back home he couldn't walk right. His rear end fishtailed. When he jumped off the bed he fell and crashed in a most clumsy fashion. The doctors we saw said that Louie was not in pain. Louie still can't walk or jump like a normal cat. But he's a great climber. And a great cat!

Whenever a medication or operation is recommended, ask why it is necessary, what the potential side effects or complications could be, and what your other options are. Because the cost of long-term treatment or illness can become a burden, don't be ashamed to ask about the price of these treatments.

Ask your veterinarian not to hold your cat by the scruff of his neck unless absolutely necessary. If you're not happy with how your cat is treated or handled, look for another vet.

If you have a choice, bring your cat home after treatment instead of letting him stay overnight. Being away from home is stressful for cats.

When your cat is back in his carrier, give him another treat and praise him.

Most cats don't fight the veterinarian. If your cat becomes a nightmare at the vet's, it could be that the veterinarian isn't the right one for that cat.

If your veterinarian recommends an expensive or drastic procedure, shop around for a second opinion.

When You Get Home

Doctor visits usually will wear your cat out for the rest of the day, especially if he gets vaccines. Don't expect him to be too chipper. Allow him outside for a short walk unless his condition prohibits that. Fix a wet meal when he comes back into the house. He'll be tired and soon will be ready for a very long nap.

Handle your cat gently for the first twenty-four hours after any shot. If he shows signs of pain or fever after a shot, call the veterinarian immediately.

16

Administering Treatments

🐾 There's no reason to struggle after the veterinarian sends you home with some unpleasant instructions and medication for your cat. In this chapter, I'll give you tips to help you deal with giving pills, applying eye ointments, cleaning ears, and taking her temperature.

Treatment Tips

● The best time to give treatments is when your cat is tired or hungry; cats tend to be least resistant then.

● Have the medicine and a special treat ready in your pocket, and all the supplies (pills, swabs, drops, etc.) ready at hand before you get your cat and start treatment.

● Never sound or act angry. While you're giving the cat his treatment, talk softly to him. Handle him firmly enough for him to know

Shopping List

✓ special food treats or a wet meal for afterward
✓ towel or blanket for your cat to sit on
✓ KY jelly, Vaseline, or massage oil for thermometer
✓ flexible digital thermometer
✓ cotton swabs for ear cleaning
✓ butter or oil for pill
✓ alcohol to clean thermometer
✓ and don't forget the medicine!

See the Products and Resources section in the Appendix for more information.

that you mean business, but gently and compassionately enough for him to trust you.

- If he resists, comfort him with petting or distract him with a toy and then try again. If you still don't succeed, wait until he's been still for a second or two and then let him go. Try again in a few minutes.
- After any treatment, give him praise and a treat. Try to make him forget the awful injustices done to his body!
- Pet him and pay attention to him several times a day other than just when giving him his treatment. Don't let him think that every time you approach him it's to give him medicine.

Pills

If the doctor says your cat's pills can be crushed and given with food, you're in luck. Simply mash the pill into little bits and stir into a bit of wet food.

If the pill must go down whole, coat it with butter or oil. Hide it in your hand. Approach the cat gently while she's still in bed and sleepy. Hold the pill between your thumb and forefinger. Pry her mouth open and quickly drop the pill as far back on her tongue as you can. If it sticks on her tongue, use a pencil to knock the pill to the back of her throat. Close her mouth; this forces her to swallow the pill.

If the pill pops out, pick it up right away and try again. Don't hesitate, or she will start to squirm and fight. As soon as the event is over, distract her with the usual praise, petting, and treats.

Eye Ointments

It's easiest if you start while your cat is sleeping. After washing your hands, gently hold her head. With the ointment in your right hand, pull the upper lid up with your left thumb and pull the lower lid down with the little finger of your right hand. Slowly squeeze the recommended dosage along the inside of the lower lid. Let her blink to spread the ointment along her eyelids. Then offer endless praise.

Cleaning Ears

If your cat has ear mites, your veterinarian will give you a solution to use to clean her ears. This will take a couple of treatments per day, during which your cat must be still for longer than most cats are comfortable with.

Because drops fling out when a cat shakes its head, I usually clean ears in the bathroom. Before you begin, have a towel for your cat to sit on, cotton swabs, the ear medication, and some treats. Take the cat into the bathroom and shut the door.

true story

Sam was my beloved cat for more than fourteen years. For many of those years, I believed the only way anyone could clean a cat's ears was to wrap him in a blanket first.

Eventually, I realized that Sam wasn't struggling with me because he was getting his ears cleaned; he struggled with me because I was wrapping him up. When I started just holding his ear while I talked to him, the cleaning would last long enough to get the job done—on both ears.

Clean her ears as recommended by the veterinarian, usually by putting a few drops of the solution into the ears, massaging with your finger, and then swabbing the excess out with cotton swabs. Be very careful not to insert the swab too far into her ear canal.

She'll instinctively try to scratch her ears while you're cleaning them. You can go ahead and let her do that while you continue to clean. Just be careful to stay away from her claws.

If she starts to squirm, stop for a second or two and start again. Cleaning really dirty ears can take quite a while, so you might plan on cleaning just one ear at a time. And if she starts to struggle too much, you can quit for now and continue later. Her ears are done when the swab comes out clean.

Taking Your Cat's Temperature

A cat's temperature is taken using a rectal thermometer. Flexible, digital thermometers provide a fast and accurate reading. They even beep to let you know when you can take them out. I don't recommend conventional mercury thermometers because they do not bend, require about five minutes of insertion before reading, and if it should break, the mercury is dangerous to both person and cat.

Apply a bit of Vaseline, KY jelly, or massage oil to the thermometer before insertion. Tell her she's being good while you massage her body and work your way toward her hip area. Gently insert the thermometer. Stroke her and say her name as long as she isn't resisting. If she starts to struggle, hold her firmly and speak in a tone that makes her understand that she's not going anywhere until you're done.

Swab the thermometer with rubbing alcohol afterward. Whatever type of thermometer you use, write "Cat Use Only" on it, and restrict its use accordingly.

Yucky Stuff

Sooner or later, everybody's cat produces some form of yucky stuff: vomit, hairballs, diarrhea, and poop. The way I see it, learning how to deal with these vile substances is just part of the job.

Vomit

Cats often give warning signs that they are about to vomit, whether what's coming up is food or hairballs. Some cats will "yowl" once or twice shortly before throwing up. Sometimes they'll run around the house very fast while drooling and smacking their tongue on their lips. Or they'll begin to dry heave and convulse, a sure sign that vomit will soon appear. If you notice any of these, immediately put a newspaper under him or move him to a noncarpeted area before he does the deed. But

Shopping List

✓ carpet cleaner
✓ rags, sponges, or paper towels
✓ hairball remedy, such as Cat-Lube Hairball & Digestive Aid or Hair Ball Gel (See Products and Resources in the Appendix)
✓ dietary fiber

Optional

✓ brown rice
✓ low sodium chicken broth
✓ cottage cheese
✓ ascorbic acid crystals (vitamin C)
✓ "kitty oats" or "kitty grass" seeds

See the Products and Resources section in the Appendix for more information.

121

you have to move fast. I rarely get to my cats in time, so I keep carpet cleaners and sponges on hand.

Cats often vomit after eating too much too fast, or eating something that doesn't agree with them. There also may be a medical problem, such as FUS (feline urologic syndrome), or poisoning.

 Helpful Hint ■ When my cats eat grass outside, I wait until they throw up out there before letting them back in the house.

If you think your cat is eating too fast, feed him smaller servings more frequently. Also, help slow him down by spreading out his regular serving on a larger plate.

If your cat vomits after he eats a certain brand or variety of food, change to something different, or try lesser amounts of what he's been eating.

Your cat also may be having trouble with certain kinds of meat. If, for example, he's been upchucking beef, try a different meat, such as lamb or chicken. Or try raw or homemade food (see Chapter 12).

Medical problems and poisoning are best left for the veterinarian to treat. To rule out medical problems or poisoning, you need to call your veterinarian.

Hairballs

Cats ingest loose hair as they groom themselves. The hair collects in the stomach and must occasionally be coughed up or excreted in his poop. Sometimes hair gets stuck in his throat, which can lead to a dry cough.

Hairballs are the same size and shape as poop. It's easy for a cat owner to mistake the two. Hairballs, however, have a different texture and color. If you were to try to "separate" your cat's stool, it wouldn't separate. It would be sticky and would stay clumped together, just as human stools do.

While hairballs are yucky, they serve a useful function. If the hair builds up for too long in the cat's stomach, he may not be able to cough it up or pass it through. This can result in a very, very sick cat.

The first step you should take is to make sure that you brush your cat regularly to reduce the amount of hair he swallows. Then try these suggestions to help your cat get rid of the hair he does ingest:

- Hairball remedies, which can be found in pet stores, mail-order catalogs, and veterinarians' offices, will make it easier for your cat to pass his hair in his stool. Many cats will lick the gooey substance directly from the tube or container. If yours won't, rub some on his leg for him to lick off. Use a small glob, or he'll shake the excess off and get stuff on your walls. You also can rub the substance into his hair with the nozzle of the applicator. Buy hairball remedies that don't contain sugar or benzoate of soda, which is a preservative.

- Half a teaspoon of butter once or twice a week also can help him pass the hair in his stool. For over a century, my mother, my grandmother and I have fed our cats butter (no margarine) or lawn grass for hairball remedies. Rub it on his paws or let him lick it off a plate.

- Add fiber in powder or tablet form to his diet. Fiber supplements are available at pet stores, health food stores, or through mail order. Follow the directions on the package.

- For additional fiber, grow "kitty oats" or "kitty grass" indoors. (See Products and Resources in the Appendix.) Cats will nibble on the young shoots. Catnip is another source of fiber.

- If he's coughing, try rubbing his neck and shoulders; it seems to help.

- Take him outdoors. Eating grass in the yard will help your cat throw up the hair—and the grass will come up with it. Keep your cat away from lawns that have been treated with weed killers for as long as the manufacturer recommends.

Diarrhea

Cat diarrhea looks like melted chocolate and smells really bad. If your cat has a diarrhea problem, pay attention to what he's eating. Milk is a common culprit. Remove suspected food from his diet, and vary the diet so that he doesn't have more of any one particular food than he can handle.

There also are certain foods that can improve the consistency of your cat's stools. Try giving him:

- Homemade meals
- Organic catnip
- Cooked brown rice or brown rice cereal
- Cheese or cottage cheese
- Blueberries
- Low sodium chicken broth with a pinch of ascorbic acid (vitamin C)
- Dietary fiber recommended for hairballs, which also can help prevent diarrhea

If your cat continues to have diarrhea problems, call the veterinarian.

 WARNING ▦ Don't let your cat out into the yard if weed killer, garden supplement, or pesticide was recently applied.

Poop

Cats shouldn't poop outside the litter box. If you think your cat is pooping outside the litter box, look again. The little gifts could be coughed-up hairballs. Remember that they resemble each other, so look carefully.

When you've determined he's really pooping outside of the litter box, consider the following.

- He may be constipated. Add more moisture and fiber to his diet with homemade meals, table scraps, and canned food. For additional fiber, include catnip and kitty oats. Provide at least two wet meals each day to help keep his "internals" moist. If the problem continues, stop feeding dry food altogether. Laxative-based hairball remedies also can help relieve constipation.
- Switch to a litter that doesn't contain sodium bentonite as a clumping agent. If ingested, it can contribute to constipation problems.
- Clean the litter box. It may be too dirty. Cats are tidy creatures. Some will poop outside, yet near, the box if it is too dirty.

 WARNING ■ Call the veterinarian immediately if your kitten has diarrhea. Diarrhea causes dehydration, which can quickly kill a kitten. If an adult cat has diarrhea for more than two days, call the veterinarian.

Part 3
Cat Behavior

129	18 ●	Basic Training
138	19 ●	Outside/Inside
153	20 ●	Aggression
162	21 ●	Litter Box Blues
179	22 ●	Miscellaneous Problems

18

Basic Training

🐾 No matter where Louie is—even if he's asleep, hiding, or outside—he comes running when he hears me call "Here, Louie!" It's because I put my cats through "basic training," which is easier than it sounds. I don't use squirt bottles or clickers. I simply talk to my cats and tell them, and sometimes ask them, to do what I want them to do. And they do it.

Cats *will* listen. They *will* come when called. (White cats often are deaf, but most cats aren't hard of hearing.) They'll even learn tricks and hand signals if you want them to.

Basic training builds strong and useful communication links between you and your cat. In this chapter, you'll learn the three rules of basic training:

1. Never hit him. Trust is necessary for training. Hitting will not teach a cat to trust you.
2. Be aware of how to talk to him. Only say his name when he's good. Never use his name with "No."

Shopping List

✓ cat toys
✓ cat brush
✓ catnip
✓ food treats

Optional

✓ empty soda can with a few pennies in it (put tape over the opening on the can)

See the Products and Resources section in the Appendix for more information.

---

3. *Always* make it a pleasure for him to come to you or to come home. No matter what.

Also, throughout the book, I give suggestions on how to reward and reprimand certain good or bad behavior, such as scratching post training and aggression.

Rewards

Rewards are a necessary part of training. Reprimands only teach a cat what *not* to do. Rewards should be reserved for reinforcing good behavior. Sometimes a cat owner does not know that he or she actually is rewarding bad behavior. A popular example is when a cat is mean to another cat—the bully often gets the attention when it's the victim that should be getting it all.

When the cat does something good, he needs to be recognized. Any attention or recognition given to him is a reward.

Rewards can be anything the cat likes. It can be a "great" reward, such as food and going outside, or something as simple and quick as a pet or kind word. Playing with a lure toy or being massaged or brushed also may be favorite rewards.

 Cats Are Like People ■ We appreciate sincerity. Hearing a sincere "Hello" or "I'm sorry" can make a big difference in our attitude.

Another reward is simply to say your cat's name anytime he's good. You want to always have him know that when he hears his name, he is being good. Cut down on his guesswork. "Mommy said my name. I *must* be doing something good or she wouldn't have said it!" Don't say his name when what you mean is "I'm warning you." And don't say his name when he's being a jerk.

Rule number three says to always make it a pleasure for your cat to come to you or to come home. This means that if your cat even simply walks to you, don't do something he thinks is bad, such as giving him a pill, taking him indoors, or trimming a nail. If you must do something "bad" to your cat, go to him. And let your cat know he's welcomed home. Even if he was gone for several hours, and even if he got in a cat fight outside, give him a treat and sound pleased to see him as soon as he's in the house.

Food Treats As Rewards

Food treats are listed in Chapter 12. Reserve food treats for when he's been through something difficult. Besides making him feel better, this helps prevent stress-related behavior problems. I also use a wet meal, which is Louie's daily treat, to reinforce the "Here, Louie" command.

Unless he's really super-old, it's best not to give food treats for no rhyme or reason. Indiscriminate treats can start nasty habits, like nagging and bugging you for little tidbits throughout the day.

Good Times to Give a Food Treat

▶ When your cat gets into his carrier for a trip to the veterinarian, while at the vet's office, and for the trip home

▶ After cleaning his ears or giving him medicine or other home treatments

▶ When he comes when called under stress

▶ Always when he comes home! (Or plan his wet meal for the end of his walk)

▶ To a senior citizen cat, daily, just because he's old

Reprimands

A loud, simple "No" is about the only reprimand you'll need to use. Just say "No!" Do *not* say his name when you use the word "no." But even "no" must be used with caution; use only as much force in the word "no" as the cat can handle. Some cats are easily offended.

Say "No" quickly in response to his walking on the counter, jumping on the stove, or scratching the sofa (but don't start reprimanding for scratching the sofa until positive use of the scratching post has been ingrained for a few weeks). If he still doesn't stop, say "No" again and loudly clap twice. Keep at him until he stops— even if you have to push him off the stove or counter or pick him up and carry him to his scratching post. He needs to know you mean business.

As soon as your cat stops doing the misbehavior, tell him he's a good boy. Whenever a cat is *not* doing something bad, he is being good. It does not matter if he was bad just five seconds ago; if he's good right this very second, he needs to hear "Good boy!"

Do not feed a cat or let him outside after seriously poor behavior, such as spraying or urinating. It's okay to tell him he's a good boy a few minutes later; just don't feed him special food in the next half hour. Unless he lives outside, do not put him outside in response to his soiling the house. A cat will learn to do those things to be let outside.

Helpful Hints ■ Get him more used to doing things that you ask of him. When you think he's in the mood to do what you want, ask him if that's what he'll do, such as "Time to scratch" or "Here, Louie!" The more choices he thinks he's allowed to make, the more he'll make the ones you want him to, when you want him to.

Sound happy to see him. Saying his name and "Hey, where you been, man?" can make him feel special.

If he stops misbehaving before you can say "No," don't say it. It's too late. In fact, depending on the situation and the type of misbehavior, you might want to praise him for stopping. For example, if he starts to jump on the counter and you look his way and he refrains, praise him.

It's very important to consistently respond to bad behavior. If you don't want him on the counter, you need to say "No" *every* time you see it happen. Sometimes, cats will intentionally break rules just to see if you will be lazy today. Don't let it go "just this once" or he will try longer and harder tomorrow. Once your cat learns that "no" means "no," he often will learn that something is off-limits by being told just a few times.

Basic Training Tips

▶ *Never* reprimand him for peeing outside his box.

▶ Never use your cat's name when giving a reprimand. Only use his name when giving praise, or calling him, or just talking with him. That way, he'll always associate his name with something good.

▶ If you know your cat is about to misbehave, distract him with petting or a toy. Or simply talk to him and say his name to divert his mischief.

▶ Never reprimand him when he walks to you, or comes home. Always make coming home, or coming to you, a good and trustworthy experience.

Scaring the cat also can be a reprimand. If your cat continues to jump the fence or onto the counter, set up a situation in which you can catch him at it without being seen. When he does it, scare him by throwing a can of pennies or making a loud noise from where you're hiding. He is more likely to stop this behavior if he thinks he can't get away with it even when he's alone.

WARNING ▪ Never reprimand a cat for urinating outside his box. That is like punishing a child for wetting the bed. See Chapter 21, Litter Box Blues.

Reserve the word "no" to mean *never*. When he wants something that he can't have right now, say "Not now" or something like that. He's not being bad; he may just be whining. If you tell him "not now," enforce it. Do not give in until well after the cat has forgotten what it was he had wanted.

Sometimes ignoring the cat can act as a reprimand. When a cat is acting like a bully or being foolish, give attention to the cats who *are* behaving well. Don't even look him in the eye until he's acting more civilized.

Scruffing

Scruffing is controlling a cat by grabbing and holding the loose skin at the base of his neck. Mother cats scruff their kittens to carry them, but being scruffed is humiliating and frightening to an adult cat.

Only scruff your cat when there is danger of injury to you or someone else, or to the cat himself. While he's being scruffed, support his hind end with the other hand. Limit the scruff hold to as little time as possible, releasing the grip as soon as the danger has passed. In Chapter 19 you will see scruffing mentioned as a last-resort reprimand to be used if the cat crosses the street. That is the only time in this book that I recommend using scruffing as a reprimand. If you have to do it more than twice, the outside training is not worth continuing. Scruffing needs to be reserved for emergency stuff.

 Helpful Hint ■ Don't say "no" when he scratches or bites. Say "Ouch" instead. (See Chapter 20 for more about aggression.)

Don't Hit Him or Squirt Him

Do not hit, spank, or otherwise hurt your cat as a way to deter bad behavior. Hitting only teaches your cat to fear you and run away from you. Hitting does not teach a cat what is expected of him and does not encourage him to trust people or their hands.

Getting sprayed with water is a traumatic experience for a cat, and it should be done only to break up a serious cat fight. Spraying water may also be used to interrupt or distract your cat in a life-threatening situation such as crossing the street or trespassing into an angry neighbor's yard. Keep a spray bottle or squirt gun on your back porch, or wherever else a serious confrontation is likely to occur.

Training Your Cat to Come When Called

It's really nice to have your cat come to you when you want him to. And it helps to make other training much easier.

"Here, Louie!"

That's all I have to say, and Louie comes running, even outdoors on a nice day. You can train your cat the same way I train mine to come when I call.

Start feeding him his wet meals at the same time every day. When he shows up to eat, say "Here" with his name even if he's only a few feet away. When he reaches you, say "Good boy [his name]" and place the meal in front of him. Pet him and let him eat. Do this with every meal or special treat that you give him. Soon, he will associate your call with eating and will be very motivated to show up.

Helpful Hints

▶ I say "Hello, Louie!" when he enters the room. I say "I'm sorry, Louie," when it is my fault that he ran into me.

▶ Ask your cat what he wants, and then follow him to where he leads you.

When your cat comes dependably for his wet meals, start calling him when he's a few feet away. Graduate to calling when he's in another room. Choose times when he's walking toward you and likely to reach you. This helps build habit and success. Say "Here" with his name. Pet him and then feed him when he arrives.

Rewards for Good Behavior

▶ Food treat
▶ A trip outside
▶ Play time with you
▶ Catnip
▶ Petting
▶ Praise (say his name!)

Make him earn his food by allowing you to touch him before he gets his meal. When he's doing pretty well on coming to you from short distances, start calling him at unexpected times, such as naps, but do this only when he's going to get a really good reward, such as his afternoon walk or his favorite toy.

true story

A month after getting my new cat, Lincoln, my husband and his friends accidentally let him out after dark. They didn't even know Lincoln was missing until I went looking for him. I was frantic when I couldn't find him because he had not yet been trained for being outdoors. I went outside with a flashlight and saw some movement in the neighbor's yard. I had spent a month saying "Here, Lincoln" with his wet meals and was hoping it would pay off now.

I knelt down and called "Here, Lincoln!" He was about thirty feet away and he came to me—in the dark, his first time out in the yard ever! I made a big deal of how good he was and lavished him with hugs, kisses, and food. (As you will learn in Chapter 19, a cat that responds to your calling his name usually should be rewarded with a longer yard stay. However, this nighttime episode was a special circumstance.)

P.S. After this incident, I wanted to put my husband, Bruce, out after dark and "forget" about him!

P.P.S. After this incident, I would not allow my husband's band to practice at our house for the next three years. I finally forgave Bruce. After all, he is the best cook, singer, and piano player in the world!

Say the same words in the same style every time so that he becomes conditioned to expect only good things anytime he hears that particular tone and combination.

In the first few months, do not pick up or hold a cat that comes to your call. Let him walk freely on the ground unless he asks you specifically to be picked up. The more you let a cat have his freedom when he comes when called, the more likely it is that he'll walk to you again. As time goes by, he may not mind being picked up and held, even when he didn't ask.

After your cat is coming for wet meals, he'll be ready for a few nonfood rewards when you call him. Use whatever your cat is enticed by: praise and petting, play, massage, catnip, or a walk outside. Continue to say "Here" with his name before wet meals every day.

Did You Know? ■ A cat will walk in the direction of whatever he wants. Whether it's play, food, or outside walks, he'll walk in that direction and stay in the area where he gets those things while looking directly in your eyes. If he walks to you and stays near you, he probably wants to be petted and massaged. When he hurriedly walks away from you, he's most likely trying to show you what he wants.

He'll also hang out where he was last brushed or played with to see if he'll get brushed or played with again. He'll look at you and then look at his brush or toy.

Most cats, when they are Out want to be In, and vice versa, and often simultaneously.

Dr. Louis J. Camuti, DVM

Outside/Inside

When I take Louie and Marvin on their outside walks, they stay in the yard and come when called. They run to the house when they see cars and strangers, and walk back into the house of their own accord. I don't have to chase them down or carry them all over the place, because I taught them to behave outside.

Some shelters insist that the people who adopt cats from them not let them outside. I can understand that. They've seen lots of lost, stolen, injured, and dead cats, all because of outside hazards. But you can take your cat outside in relative safety by teaching him to avoid danger *and* stay in the yard.

Trained outside walks can benefit both you and your cat in many ways:

- Walking and fresh air help relieve stress and will make your cat more stress tolerant.
- Because he will be familiar with his surroundings, he'll know where to go in the event that he accidentally gets outside.
- Allowing your cat to go outdoors is a great way to reward him for using the scratching post and for coming when called.
- Being outdoors often alleviates or stops a cat's worst behavior problems—problems that result in some cats being mistreated, abandoned, or euthanized.

Shopping List

For Outside Walks

- ✓ brightly colored cat collar with safety release, bell, and your phone number (write the phone number with permanent ink or add a tag)
- ✓ cat harness, such as the narrow web, 3/8-inch-wide Surefit Harness that our cat, Mr. Abraham Lincoln, prefers (see Products and Resources in the Appendix)
- ✓ lightweight leash
- ✓ industrial squirt bottle and/or Super Soaker squirt gun
- ✓ cat treats or wet cat food
- ✓ microchip implant (call your veterinarian or local shelter)

Optional:

- ✓ empty soda pop can with pennies inside (put tape over the opening)

- ✓ cat tattooed with registered number (strongly recommended)

For indoor-only cats:

- ✓ kitty oats (grown indoors)
- ✓ hairball remedy
- ✓ extra cat tree / scratching post
- ✓ catnip
- ✓ extra litter box
- ✓ raw foods

Optional:

- ✓ bird feeder
- ✓ outdoor cat kennel
- ✓ *The City Cat,* by Roz Riddle
- ✓ *The Indoor Cat,* by Patricia Curtis

See the Products and Resources section in the Appendix for more information.

As a cat owner consultant, I don't recommend adopting a cat unless you are able to give the cat time outside. Some cats go crazy when they are kept indoors only; others develop physical ailments. Taking a cat outside relieves you from having to provide the daily requirements of fun, entertainment, vitamin D (from sunshine), dirt, and grass that a cat needs to be mentally and physically healthy. Going outside is the cheapest yet most interesting cat "baby sitter" you will ever find. Boredom causes bad behavior in cats. But when outside, cats can watch birds, sniff bushes, and enjoy fresh air for hours. Safe time spent outdoors is *the best* entertainment, and stress and pain reliever that a cat can possibly receive.

The Right Circumstances for Training?

Supervised outside walks can be fun and very beneficial to cats and cat owners, but only if you have the proper cat, the proper setting, and time.

Not just any cat can be taken on outside walks. If your cat likes to fight or has been brought up in the streets, he may not take to this type of training well. Try keeping him in the house for several months. Then, if possible, begin training on an exceptionally cold day so that he'll only want to be out for a few minutes.

Warning ■ Don't take your cat outside:
- ▶ At dark or near dark (twilight)
- ▶ When there's a moving van or a vehicle with a trunk or window left open and unattended nearby
- ▶ On these holidays or the day before: Halloween, New Year's Eve, Fourth of July, Cinco de Mayo, or any other holiday that's celebrated with firecrackers
- ▶ Right after any misbehavior (going outside should be a favorite reward; don't reward bad behavior)
- ▶ If weed killer or garden supplement has recently been applied (contact manufacturer to find out when the lawn will be safe for pets)

If the cat is an extremely fast runner, or doesn't like to be touched or held, he won't be a good candidate for outside walks. If you live near heavy traffic or you don't have a yard, you probably should keep your cat indoors. (I have, however, known of many cats that lived on busy streets to the age of more than twenty years.) You also should not let your cat outside if there are predatory animals around. (See the Indoor-Only Cat section at the end of this chapter.)

If you have a kitten, consider keeping the kitten indoors for about a year to get him very used to routine. This can really help keep him closer to home when he goes on walks.

Outdoor training will start at about five minutes per day. The time the cat will stay outside depends on how much he violates your orders during certain phases of training. Try to do outside walks daily. If you can only take your cat outside during the weekend, you may have a problem if he is declawed. Once a declawed cat gets used to outside walks, he may require one every day. The stress of being inside may make the cat pee outside the litter box. If you can't walk a declawed cat daily, you may not want to start this training.

Helpful Hints

▶ Choose only one door of the house to let your cat out of. It's easier to manage just one door.

▶ Allow the cat to walk inside through any door.

▶ If your home has other doors he can go out of, don't let your cat use the front door. You'll then have less trouble with your cat when it comes time for you to use that door for visitors.

▶ If he gets out of the door on his own without your permission, get him back inside the house as soon as possible. Don't let him get away with it even once.

Training

The attitude you must convey to your cat is that going outside is his privilege, not his right. This training is geared for that attitude.

Ideally, your cat should live inside the house for quite a few months before you begin outside training. You need to make the cat or kitten dependent upon you before going outside. During this time, feed wet meals at the same time each day so he learns when to expect them. (This will help with outside training because cats are creatures of habit—if they're used to being fed at the same time every day, they'll come inside, even if the weather is nice.) Also, train him to come when called, as explained in Basic Training (Chapter 18).

Outside training requires a harness, a leash, and a collar with a bell. I also highly recommend tattooing and a microchip for any cat that goes out. (See Products and Resources in the Appendix.)

Before You Begin

There are a number of things you should do before you actually begin the process of training:

- Let your neighbors know that you have a cat and that you will be training him to stay in your yard. Tell them that your cat is not allowed in anybody's yard but his own, and that they can either shoo him away if he goes into their yards or call and let you know he's there.
- Check to see that your cat's rabies vaccinations are up to date. Your local laws may require additional vaccines as well.
- If you don't have a fence, set up some flags or stones to mark the boundaries that your cat is to stay within.
- Get a lure toy that you can leave outside. Later on it will come in handy to literally "lure" your cat back inside the house.

true story

I kept Marvin in the house for a whole year before beginning outside training. Delaying his outdoor privileges made him more cautious and willing to stay pretty close to home.

- Keep a spray bottle handy to stop cat fights. Children's pump-up squirt guns or industrial spray bottles are my favorites. The Super Soaker shoots pretty far. The longer stream lets you hide behind the bushes, waiting to ambush your cat when he violates the rules. You may need to station a spray bottle or two around the house as a backup arsenal. You'll use water later in the training. As previously mentioned, it's best to avoid spraying water at your cat's head. But if your cat gets into a serious situation where his action *must* be interrupted (such as crossing the street when a car is near) then waste no time in trying to avoid squirting his head.
- Stick to a single session each day during the first several months or your cat will pester you until you take him out a second time,

then a third, and so on. Later you'll be able to take him outside more than once a day if you want. But for now, he needs to respect the time he gets to spend outside.

● To avoid having your cat wake you up for his outside walk, wait until after you've been awake a couple of hours to take him out. Always take him out during daylight, never at night or in the twilight.

Phase One

Phase one takes about three days. Its purpose is to give the cat a good first impression of the outdoors. For this phase, pick a quiet time so that the cat is less overwhelmed. Also, choose a time shortly before your cat usually takes a nap, because at that time he'll be tired and more likely to stay close to home. For most cats this seems to be between 10:00 A.M. and 3:00 P.M. Later, you'll take him out at noisier and busier times.

When it's time to go out, call "Here!" with his name, even if he's already by the door. Praise him while you put his harness and leash on him. Make sure he's also wearing a collar with a bell, just in case he slips out of the harness.

Tell him it's time to go outside but that it's also "Time to scratch." Put him on his scratching post. As soon as he scratches his post, praise him as you pick him up and carry him through the doorway. (You need to carry him so he knows you're in control. This also will change later.) Set him down facing the house a few feet outside the door. Pet him now so that right away he starts getting used to being touched while he's outside.

Let him walk around and sniff at things while you keep hold of his leash. *Every few minutes, go to him, pick him up, pet him, say his name, and put him down facing the house.* This helps avoid teaching the cat to run from you. He will learn to run and hide if you take him inside as soon as you get your hands on him. Remember, first impressions are important, so start getting him used to being handled and approached right away. You want to be able to touch or pick up your cat anytime he's outside.

Don't drag him by the leash and harness; if you do, he'll learn to escape. Cats can escape most harnesses. Once a cat learns that he can get out of one, he'll escape all the time. Stay close by so that you can get your hands on him at any given time. It's okay to step on the leash should he suddenly bolt away from you, but grab him immediately (the harness won't hold him). If he bolts, puts your hands on him and see if he'll calm down. If he's ready to run off again, take him inside. Give him a treat and try again tomorrow. It's not a good idea to take a cat inside as soon as you get your hands on him while he's in his own yard, but bolting needs to be discouraged until he learns the yard boundaries.

Praise him whenever he walks toward the house or you. Play with him near the house using the lure toy you've been keeping on the porch. Let him know that staying near to or going in the house is a good thing.

Keep the sessions short and avoid letting him near the yard boundary for these first three days. You don't want to have to say "no" during this part of the training.

 WARNING ▪ Do not leave him unattended while he's wearing a harness. Never depend on a harness to restrain your cat.

Later on, he'll learn to come back indoors on his own. For now, though, you need to keep his outside walk short because he's not likely to walk in on his own. You'll have to pick him up. Don't call him when it's time to go in; instead, go to him and pick him up. If the cat stays calm in your arms, carry him around for several seconds before you take him in so that he doesn't associate getting picked up with going inside. If he gets antsy, however, take him in immediately.

As soon as he's inside, praise him and then remove his harness, leash, and bell. Tell him how good he is to be home. Give him a treat or serve a wet meal if it's mealtime. Coming home always deserves a special food treat, no matter how he acted outside.

Most cats love the outdoors, but some are frightened by it at first. Your cat may act as if he doesn't like the outside at all. If he freaks out once he gets outside, try using a lure toy to distract him from his fear. Don't talk to him unless he loosens up or wants to go back in the house. Then open the door, praise him, and let him slink inside. Tell him how good he is to come inside no matter how scaredy-cat he seems. Give him a treat and try phase one again for the next day or two. If he doesn't like it any better, don't force it. Let him stay indoors. See the Indoor-Only Cat section later in this chapter.

Phase Two

In this phase he'll learn where the property lines exist and that if he crosses them too much, it will stop his walk for the day. He'll also come to understand that walking to you or staying on his own turf earns him extra time outside.

Gradually change his walk to a busier and noisier time of the day. This will make him more aware of the dangers outside. Sometimes the commotion alone will make him stay near the house. Ideally, you should time the training sessions to end right before it's time for a wet meal.

Begin by taking your cat outside just as in phase one. But this time, after you set him down outside and pet him, let go of the leash. Let him go wherever he wants. And again, as in phase one, every few minutes, go to him and pick him up, pet him, and set him back down again, facing the house.

Whenever he gets near the yard boundary, watch closely and stay near him. The instant he steps on the sidewalk or outside any boundary, say "No." Stop him from going farther by walking in front of him, and gently force him back into his yard by pushing him *lightly* with your hand. If he won't get back into his own yard, pick him up and return him to just inside his property line. Say "Good boy" as soon as he's back in bounds.

Stay close to him as he roams around the yard. If he approaches the line again, say something like "Uh-uh," or "Hey! I'm watching you," but do not say his name. If he crosses the boundary again, then again put him back inside his yard. Take him inside if he crosses a third time.

Helpful Hints ▦ When he walks up to you on his own, pet him and praise him. Pick him up if he wants you to. Let him go again for at least a few minutes, even if it's time to come in. You always want to reward his coming to you. Open the door and give him a chance to go back in the house on his own.

A good time to take a cat inside the house is when you catch him in someone else's yard and he makes no attempt to run to you or run back home. If he runs back into his yard before you can catch him, let him stay out a little bit longer. Remember, don't take him inside when he walks to you. When he walks up to you, tell him he's a very good boy and pet him.

If it's time to go inside and he doesn't walk in on his own, try a lure toy to lure him indoors, and then continue to play with him once he's inside. Or, you could tell him it's time to eat. When all else fails, silently walk to him, pick him up, and carry him around for a few seconds. Then apologize for taking him inside. As soon as he's indoors, let him go gently, pet and praise him, and give him a treat.

Your cat will need to make mistakes on all sides of the yard in order to learn where the boundaries are. He'll need to experience being yelled at, gently pushed, and carried back from all sides of your property.

Make sure you respond each time he trespasses, either by putting him back in the yard or taking him in the house. Letting him get away with it without making him get back in his own yard can set the training back a few weeks.

Whenever you call for him outside, have his most special food ready, or a very favorite toy. Praise him as soon as he shows up, even if it's ten minutes after you first called. Use special rewards after he comes to you when you call for him outside.

If he tries to bolt on several days during this phase, he may not be a good candidate for this training. Keeping him inside the house for a year, and getting him to come to you when called during that time, may help break his need to run. If your cat is the type that is too outgoing and curious to be kept in one yard, training him to walk with you on a harness around the neighborhood is another option.

Most cats will learn where the yard boundaries are. When he continues to hesitate before crossing them for several days in a row, he's waiting to see if you're paying attention. So you know he knows, start cutting down to only allowing two mistakes for a week or two.

And now it's time for phase three.

Phase Three

In phase three you no longer need to use the leash and harness. Continue to use the collar and bell from now on whenever he's outside.

When he scratches his post after you've asked him to, you can now let him *walk* out the door without being carried.

At the beginning of this off-leash training, warn him not to trespass when he approaches a property line. Stay close. If he violates your verbal warning, even just once, take him inside right away. Try to get your hands on him as soon as he has crossed the boundary. Do this for several weeks.

As your cat gets better at staying in the yard, gradually let him go farther away from you, but keep him in sight. When he almost always respects the border while you're there, and is pretty good about coming when you call to him outside, start letting him wander out of your sight. At the least, get out of *his* sight. If you can spy on him, do so. If not, only leave for a few seconds. Gradually increase your time away to a few minutes, and then longer.

true story

Most of the time I "talk" my cats into going inside. I'll start talking to them and asking them, "What's up? Where you been, man?" Then I'll walk past my cats in the direction I want them to go (indoors). Walking ahead of them often will make them follow me. I think that's because cats like to be included in any action, and my walking ahead of them says I'm going somewhere. I'll open the door and tell them it's time to eat, and they'll walk in the house on their own.

If you find that he sneaks outside the boundaries when you aren't looking, hide from him. Then use scare tactics, such as spraying water in his path or throwing something near him the second he steps out of bounds. A snowball or an empty pop can with a few pennies inside can help startle him too (put tape over the opening on the can). If he runs back into the yard on his own, let him stay outside. If he refuses to go back to the yard, take him indoors.

As the weeks pass in phase three, you can relax again about the number of mistakes *unless* he starts making too many. If that happens, for the next few days go back to allowing only one mistake before you take him indoors for the rest of the day. Sometimes you may want to give him another chance (as I like to do on a nice sunny day). Tell him, "Get back in the yard." If he walks back into the yard on his own, let him stay out. If not, go get him with the attitude of "You should have listened to me! You thought I was joking." Then take him inside. Over time the cat will learn that you mean what you say and that staying within the property lines and walking to you earns him more time outside. The more he stays in the yard while you have your back turned, the longer you can leave him on his own. As you become more confident that he'll stay in the yard, you can just come out to check on him occasionally. It may take a few months of daily training before you can trust him to be on his own for very short periods.

When the cat walks into the house on his own, you can start to let him back outside again within a few minutes. When the weather is bad a cat will probably want in, then out, then in and out again. When you're ready to keep him inside for the day, give him his treat.

Hints to Help Him Avoid Danger ▪ Show fear when a car approaches. Say "Ooooh! Car. Be careful!" in a frightened tone of voice. Pick him up and walk quickly to the house. Put him down facing the street instead of the house so that he can look at what you are afraid of. Keep a hand on him. Sound shaky and nervous until the sound of the car disappears.

If a stranger walks by your property, be quiet but walk swiftly toward your house. Then turn around and watch until the person has gone by. Your cat will watch and pick up on your reactions. You may not want to act too scared in this case, because the stranger might think you're weird. Also, by being quiet, you won't draw unnecessary attention to a cat that's supposed to be hiding from strangers.

Once in a great while you can use scruffing as a reprimand if he crosses the *street*. (See Chapter 18 for more information about scruffing.) Save this last-resort punishment for when he continues to cross the street in spite of your warning him to not leave the yard. Carry him back to your yard and release the scruffing grip, but carry him indoors immediately. Don't forget to reward and praise him for coming home. Use this method only on very rare occasions. If your cat continues to go out into the street fairly often, try phase two again, using a harness and leash. Resorting to scruffing a cat more than twice might mean that this cat is not a good candidate for outside training.

If he leaves your yard while you're not there, praise him when he returns to the yard or door, even if he's been gone for a while.

As soon as you realize he's missing, go looking for him. Walk by the houses adjacent to your house and call his name. You may find him two houses away, and when he sees you, it's likely that he'll start running back home. Sound and act surprised and happy to see him. If he runs to you, sound extremely happy and grateful. But if he runs in the opposite direction, go after him as you say "No." Catch him and sound irritated at him until he's back inside the yard boundary. Then take him inside immediately.

As always, once your cat is back in the house, whether he was carried or walked back in, he needs to know he's always a good boy for coming home. It's time for his wet meal or treat. "Louie's home!"

true story

I tried off-and-on for seven years to train Mr. Abraham Lincoln to stay in our yard. I can't trust him—he likes to pick fights with our neighbor's gray cats, especially Gray Baby.

When I take Lincoln outside, Gray Baby shows up and then Lincoln beats him up, even though Gray Baby is the bigger cat. My other cats don't feel that way about Gray Baby—only Lincoln does. I tried keeping him inside for a year and then started outside training again, but he still was too aggressive with Gray Baby.

In October of 2003, I started taking Mr. Lincoln, then ten years old, on daily harnessed walks around the neighborhood. Within a week, his behavior drastically changed. Now he purrs more, "kneads" more, and grooms and sleeps with the other cats, which he didn't do before. Mr. Lincoln now loves to go on walks and enjoys meeting new people and dogs. Depending on the weather, we spend about an hour walking each day.

Special Considerations

Multiple Cats

If you are training more than one cat, train them outside separately until at least one of them is at the stage at which you can trust him unattended for at least five minutes. If you have to take one of them indoors, you need to be able to trust the other one while you're gone.

Declawed Cats

If you do decide to train your declawed cat to go for outside walks, try to be very regular about the training sessions. Even after phase three training, stay outside with your declawed cat. Do not leave him alone, even for a minute. Your presence provides some protection against an attack from a dog or other animal.

Indoor-Only Cat

Living indoors only is very difficult on many cats and their owners. Indoor-only cats need more attention to make up for the loss of the fun and excitement they can get from being outside in natural surroundings. Outdoors has been cats' "home" for thousands of years. Keeping a cat inside all the time is unnatural and can lead to poor health and bad behavior. Unfortunately, there are situations or cats that some owners feel must be kept inside. If that is your situation, here are some tips for keeping your indoor cat healthy and happy:

- Compensate for the lack of fresh grass by feeding him kitty oats. If you use a commercial hairball remedy, use the maximum recommended dosage. (See Chapter 17 for more on hairball remedies.)
- Add raw organic meats, vegetables, and grains to his diet at least twice a week to make up for the insects and critters he normally would eat outside. Feed mostly wet foods.
- Put cat beds in sunlit windows. A bird feeder outside the window can help him pass the time.
- Increase your play time with him, and play with him regularly.
- Let your cat jump on sturdy desks, file cabinets, bookcases, and sofas to increase his livable space. Remove breakables and

slippery things from places where the cat can jump. He may accidentally knock things down or fall after landing on something slippery.

- If your cat was used to going outside but can't now, try to ease his stress. Supplement his meals with vitamins, and give him catnip. Add an extra litter box and a new scratching post or cat tree no matter how many you already have. They're great for exercise and relieving the stress of living indoors.

- Install an outdoor kennel. Chainlink is a good material. Put a scratching post or cat tree, a dog house, and catnip plants in the kennel. If possible, install a cat door to the kennel from inside the house. Use a padlock to keep curious strangers out.

Aggression

The average healthy cat adopted from a shelter is not aggressive and should not hurt you under normal circumstances. Some cats occasionally will bite or scratch at you when irritated or handled roughly. And some may act mean toward other cats in the house or the neighbors' cats. But generally, the average healthy cat should not hurt you or others.

In this chapter I'll give you tips on how to curb aggressive behavior that's directed toward people and other cats.

> **Shopping List**
>
> ✔ large catnip-filled stuffed toy (aggression toy)
> ✔ industrial squirt bottle
> ✔ cat vitamins
>
> See the Products and Resources section in the Appendix for more information.

Causes of Aggressive Behavior

There are several possible reasons for aggressive behavior.

- *Lack of handling as a kitten:* Frequent handling of a kitten is a very important part of bringing up a friendly and gentle cat. When a kitten is not handled much or at all, he can grow up disliking being touched and preferring to be left alone. Such a cat may resist handling with a nip or a slap with his paws. A big part of behavior problems with feral cats is the lack of human handling at a critical stage in the cat's life.

- *Mistreatment or abuse:* If a cat or kitten is treated very roughly, to the point that it suffers pain and discomfort, he will learn to resist human contact.
- *Illness or injury:* Ill or injured cats, like people, can be quite irritable and even hostile. Even an innocent touch can cause pain or discomfort. A thyroid problem is just one condition known to trigger aggressive behavior in cats. Take your cat to a veterinarian to determine whether your cat's aggression is caused by being sick or injured.
- *Rough handling or play*
- *Threatening or frightening situations:* Cats are cautious creatures. Your cat may be frightened of something as obvious as a strange dog or as trivial as a slammed door. In either case, if you're holding him when he bolts, he might scratch you while trying to get away. If it's an extremely frightening situation, he might even bite.
- *Stressful living environment:* A stressed cat is more likely to bite or scratch or, more often, become skittish. Stress can be caused by many different factors. Your home may not be large enough for your family and your cats. Or it may be too noisy—certain noise levels or sounds may trigger aggressive behavior. If your cat was accustomed to regular time outside and now stays indoors, this change can cause stress.
- *Diet:* Certain foods, malnutrition, and vitamin deficiencies can trigger aggression.
- *Old age:* Old cats sometimes get grumpy. As long as he's not hurting anyone, let him growl or hiss.
- *Declawing:* Declawed cats often are quicker to bite. (See the information about declawed cats in the Special Considerations section of this chapter.)
- *Lack of exercise*
- *Boredom*

Aggressive Behavior Toward Humans

If your new kitten attacks you, it probably won't hurt. But never encourage this behavior—you don't want him to grow up thinking that climbing up people's legs is acceptable behavior. If he attacks you when he's an adult, it is definitely not cute. He must learn to attack only his own belongings.

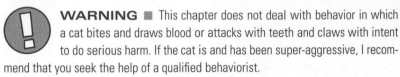 **WARNING** ▓ This chapter does not deal with behavior in which a cat bites and draws blood or attacks with teeth and claws with intent to do serious harm. If the cat is and has been super-aggressive, I recommend that you seek the help of a qualified behaviorist.

Sudden aggressive behavior could be due to abuse, a bad scare, or a medical problem. If his sudden aggression doesn't subside in a few minutes, call the veterinarian. A cat that suddenly turns aggressive might be seriously sick or injured.

Dealing with Aggression

If he just growls or hisses, simply walk away. If he actually bites you or scratches, say "Ouch!" immediately, look and sound hurt even if it really didn't hurt. Rub your bite and walk away.

If he's a kitten and you're confident that you won't get hurt, pick him up and set him down pointing away from you. Walk away. If he persists in being aggressive, lock him in the bathroom for five minutes. Have a lure toy ready and start to play with him when you let him out if he's still feeling feisty.

Watch for your cat's warning signs of anger or agitation. Pay attention to his posture so you will learn how he holds his ears and tail before he attacks. Watch his eyes and mouth. If you see an attack coming, try distracting him with a lure toy. Or push an "aggression toy" onto him. Give him something that he can kick and bite. Use a large fuzzy catnip toy or a stuffed animal sprayed with catnip. Or make your own: Stuff a tube of strong, snaggy fabric with polyester fiberfill and dried catnip. Sew the ends shut. It should be long enough for him to bite and kick at the same time. A terry-cloth sock works well.

Always handle your cat with care. Almost any cat will defend itself against rough handling. Even if your cat only scratches or bites in a rough situation, stop doing it. Rough play is not a good idea anyway. You want your cat calm and happy, not riled up. Don't use your hands to play with your cat. Use a lure toy. When cats play, they use their teeth and claws.

If your cat becomes aggressive when he hears certain noises, avoid creating those noises when you're around if possible. However, at the same time, you'll need to get the cat more used to human noise by playing music or television every day. Don't let him always be in a quiet environment. He needs to be exposed to normal human sounds to get more used to living with them.

true story

Every time I sing, Bob comes to me, cries, and nips me on the leg. If I continue to sing, he continues to nip at me until I stop singing. He doesn't exhibit this mild aggression toward any of the many singers that have sung in our home; it's only directed toward me. I won't try to change Bob's honesty—I'm a pretty bad singer. Now I sing in the shower. It sounds better in there anyway.

Add cat vitamin supplements to help alleviate moodiness. Watch his diet. Sometimes, a specific food can cause allergic reactions that can lead to angry spells. Tuna, foods that contain yeast, and hormone-injected meats have been known to do that in some cats.

Other ways to alleviate stress, and thus lessen aggression, are in Chapter 21, Litter Box Blues.

Keep his nails trimmed. Kittens' claws are sharp and will cut through your skin. Adult claws can do even more serious damage.

Do not hold a cat when he's likely to be suddenly frightened, such as when meeting a new cat or dog, walking near an appliance that's making noise, and so on.

If you get a kitten that's really aggressive and doesn't respond to training, take him back and get another. If your new adult cat is aggressive, consider returning him right away. Do not adopt a cat you think is dangerous.

Cat Fight?

Cats who live together also play together, often by pretending to fight. Just because they growl and tumble doesn't mean they're actually fighting. A serious cat fight has very quick movements, is very violent, includes high screeching sounds (not just howling), often produces blood from at least one cat, and doesn't last long. Usually, tumbling and slower movements signify playing. (Generally, I find that if either cat has a chance to walk away from the "cat fight," then it's not a true fight—they're just playing or trying to act tough.)

If your cats have had fights that aren't serious, and you would like them to get along with each other a little bit better and have more fun with each other, here are some things to do:

● While they are calm and relaxed, rub one cat and then the other. The scent from the first cat will linger on your hands. This helps get the cats more familiar with each other.

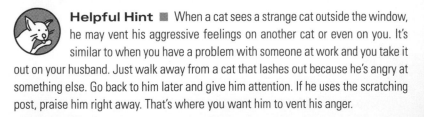

Helpful Hint ■ When a cat sees a strange cat outside the window, he may vent his aggressive feelings on another cat or even on you. It's similar to when you have a problem with someone at work and you take it out on your husband. Just walk away from a cat that lashes out because he's angry at something else. Go back to him later and give him attention. If he uses the scratching post, praise him right away. That's where you want him to vent his anger.

● For one week, put a breakaway collar *with a bell* on the most aggressive cat. This warns a more timid cat that the bully is coming.

- During mealtimes, feed the most aggressive eater first. Don't give him an additional excuse to fly off the handle.
- Cats will play by wrestling with each other. This could look like a real cat fight to someone who doesn't know that's how cats play. And they may howl and talk to each other as if it's serious. But it probably isn't. I usually just let them go on because I know they're not going to hurt each other. If I think a confrontation is growing more serious, I disrupt it by waving a lure toy to get them engaged in playing. Occasionally I may just throw a pillow near them. To further distract them, I sometimes turn on loud music before getting the toy out. But usually I just laugh off "cat fights" because I don't want to discourage interaction and play between my cats. Laughing at cat fights is often a wonderful way to distract cats from getting too serious with each other.
- If one cat is being hurt and is crying out in pain, and if you know that you won't get hurt, separate them. Pick up and comfort the cat being picked on. Ask him if he's all right. Ignore the bully. Don't say his name or make eye contact for a while. I may briefly sneer at the bully and say, "you bully!", but I then immediately return my attention back to the cat that was getting hurt to see if he is okay. If he is okay then I say, "You're okay, next time stand up to that bully, I won't always be around to defend you."

true story

When Bob and Lincoln want to start "arguing" in a room where I can close a door, sometimes I will close it. If I leave them there for an hour, they may quit arguing for quite a few weeks.

- If a fight breaks out, tell them both to "Knock it off" in a serious voice. If it looks as if one of them might get really hurt, say nothing. Use a squirt bottle. Be careful not to squirt their heads. Try to prevent fights from escalating by stepping in sooner next time.

- If you have a problem cat that is constantly bullying everyone, put him in a boarding kennel for a week. He's likely to reflect on how good his life was before he "went on vacation." When you bring him back home, confine him to a bathroom for another week. Allow him back into the household when the other cats are napping or are outside. Keep a bell on him for another week.
- If serious cat fights persist, consider finding another home for the bully. If he's not declawed, look for a place where he can be outside, too.

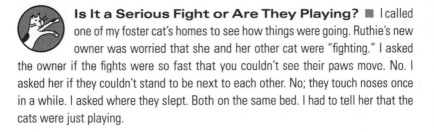

Is It a Serious Fight or Are They Playing? ▩ I called one of my foster cat's homes to see how things were going. Ruthie's new owner was worried that she and her other cat were "fighting." I asked the owner if the fights were so fast that you couldn't see their paws move. No. I asked her if they couldn't stand to be next to each other. No; they touch noses once in a while. I asked where they slept. Both on the same bed. I had to tell her that the cats were just playing.

Neighborhood Cats

Some indoor cats become agitated when they see a strange cat outside. Keep a scratching post near his favorite window. When he starts to heat up, direct him to the post. Instead of reprimanding him, tell him how brave he is for protecting the house. You may even want to place a cat bed near the window so he feels that he has an important job.

The most serious confrontations often occur when your cat is outside and unexpectedly encounters someone else's cat. Most cats try to avoid a fight, but there are a few that want to pick a fight with everything they see. If they do start fighting, break it up with a spray bottle or squirt gun. Spray the water between the brawling cats. Avoid their heads and stay as far away from the action as you can. If the fight is serious, even direct hits of water won't break it up. Keep your distance. When the fight is over, squirt at the strange cat until he's out of the yard.

Never touch a strange cat, or your own cat, when he's angry. *Also, never use any part of your body to intervene—you could be seriously hurt.* Keep your distance until things calm down. Even the most loving cat may not recognize you when he's enraged. I was viciously attacked by my own Mister Lincoln when I tried to keep him from running after Gray Booty, our neighbor's cat. When I reached for Lincoln, he scratched me badly and tried to bite me. He was too angry for me to safely touch him. I yelled to my husband to bring a blanket from the house. We threw it over Lincoln and took him back inside so he could cool off, forget about Gray Booty and think more about what he did to me! Don't make too much of a first fight. Cats get used to each other, and they may actually start to hang out together.

true story

Our Louie wouldn't hurt a soul and is very shy. But he has such a passion for playing that if another cat enters the room during his play time with me, he will attack him. Not in any serious way, but Louie isn't aggressive at any other time. (By the way, he always loses when he fights—but don't tell Louie that.)

Special Considerations

Declawed Cats

An aggression problem with a declawed cat can take longer to turn around. You may have to accept more frequent biting and other aggressive behavior for a while. But he should improve over time. To help him learn:

● Offer your hands to him when you think he won't bite. Rub his chin, but be careful; declawed cats can be moody and unpredictable. It may take several months before he learns to stop biting you (and he will learn, if he knows that you will never respond to his bites with violence or handle him roughly).

- When he bites you, say "Ouch!" and pull your hand away. If he doesn't release your hand, push it into his mouth. This forces the cat to open his mouth and release you.
- Let him hiss at other cats. If he hisses at you, walk away. If he hisses at you when you are outside, take him in immediately.

If You're Still Having Troubles

If the ideas in this chapter don't help enough with handling your cat's aggression, you may need a professional cat behaviorist. A tranquilizer also may help a cat through a stressful period in his life. Ask your veterinarian about it, or consider a new home for him where he can spend more time outside.

What Not to Do about Aggression

If you are considering declawing and/or having his teeth pulled, I urge you to reconsider. A cat without claws or teeth will be more stressed and more trouble to care for than the average cat at your local animal shelter would be.

Litter Box Blues

More than half of the phone calls I receive from cat owners are about cat urine problems. Cat urine is one of the most potent smells in the entire world. And it's no wonder that this problem causes even the best of us to have second thoughts about cats.

Cat urine can destroy practically anything. If the problem goes on long enough, the stench will permanently damage not only sofas and carpets, but even floorboards and dry wall.

If you keep a clean litter box and your cat pees outside the box, something is wrong. In this chapter I'll give you help with litter box problems and tips on how to prevent them in the future.

Shopping List

✓ visit to the veterinarian for exam; get tests
✓ cat urine neutralizer
✓ extra food bowl
✓ cat litter, different brands
✓ extra litter box or two
✓ homemade food
✓ lure toy
✓ tall, sturdy scratching post (clawed cats only)

Optional

✓ carpet runner, laundry basket
✓ large piece of cardboard or office chair mat
✓ corner litter box
✓ disposable litter boxes or cardboard boxes for litter test
✓ odor bags by Mother Nature's Odor Remover
✓ black light

See the Products and Resources section in the Appendix for more information.

Note ▓ This chapter is about the problem of your cat urinating outside of the litter box. For spraying problems, see Chapter 22; for pooping problems, see Chapter 17.

Causes of Litter Box Problems

Stress is the major cause of litter box problems. Cats get stressed out for the same reasons that people do. These reasons include:

Illness or pain. Usually the first sign that a clawed cat is sick is that he pees outside the box. Ailments such as constipation, infection, kidney stones, bad thyroid, epilepsy, depression, pain, and impacted anal glands, as well as urinary tract problems such as feline urologic syndrome (FUS), frequently cause cats to pee outside the box.

Poor diet and lack of exercise. A dry-food-only, unbalanced, or unvaried diet can contribute to kidney, liver, or bladder problems. Allergic reactions to certain foods may also prompt depression or litter box problems.

Change. Things such as keeping an outdoor cat indoors, moving to a new house, going on an extended vacation, and introducing a new dog to the household can be very stressful to some cats. Declawed cats often have a more difficult time with disruption in their daily routine and environment.

Declawing. Perhaps because declawing makes it difficult for a cat to cover its waste, declawed cats have a much higher frequency of more serious litter box problems.

Poor environment. Violence, overcrowding, loneliness, boredom, sharp smells, loud noises, or people who argue constantly all make the cat's life more stressful.

Litter box. If the box isn't kept clean or is placed in a bad location, the cat may not use it. The new electronic litter boxes, which rake the solids into a tray, may frighten and intimidate some cats to the point that they refuse to use it.

Keeping a feral cat (wild cat) in the house. Feral cats are not domesticated. If one has been used to living outside and is brought into the house, he may retaliate by peeing outside the box. It's his way of telling you he's not meant to be there.

Territorial challenges. Some cats get upset by seeing or smelling a strange cat near their home.

Bad chemistry. Not every cat fits into every home. Some cats have trouble adjusting to the wrong set of people as well as cats, dogs, or other pets.

WARNINGS
> If you are pregnant, do not handle cat litter. See Chapter 2 for more information.
> Do not reprimand a cat for peeing outside the litter box!
> If your cat cries or strains while peeing, or tries to pee more than twice in an hour, he should see a veterinarian immediately!

Preventing Litter Box Problems

The most important thing to remember is that healthy, clawed cats rarely have litter box problems. Go through this quick checklist. Is your cat:

 Eating two or three wet meals a day? Eating high-quality foods?

☑ Eating a wide variety of foods?

☑ Spending daily time with you? Getting attention every day? Cats like routine. A daily, consistent schedule for scratching post, meals, and outdoor and play time can help reduce stress and build confidence.

☑ Living with too many other cats, dogs? Overcrowding can result in territorial pressures.

☑ Getting exercise? Is he using the scratching post?

☑ Confusing heaps of dirty laundry or foul-smelling objects, such as tennis shoes, with litter boxes? Keep dirty laundry in hampers and shoes tucked away.

See the Products and Resources section in the Appendix for more information.

When Your Cat Pees Outside the Litter Box

Although there are no guaranteed cures for litter box problems, there are at least four things you can do that should help.

Take Him to the Doctor

Cats don't normally pee outside the box unless something is wrong. Even if you think the cause of the problem is that you just had a baby or moved, the onset of litter box problems may be due to illness. Never assume that the problem is "just behavioral." Too many owners mistake their cat's last veterinarian visit as a sign that Kitty is healthy because "the veterinarian saw the cat, gave his shots...the vet didn't say anything was wrong, and the cat *looks* okay." Your cat needs lab work done to confirm he doesn't have a health condition that would cause him to go outside the litter box.

Before you go to the veterinarian, inspect the litter box for the condition of your cat's stools and urine and for any blood.

If you've already been to a veterinarian, you may want to try again. Consider trying a holistic veterinarian. He or she is likely to use acupuncture, chiropractic techniques, herbs, or homeopathic home remedies to solve your cat's problem.

So that there are no surprises, call two or three different offices and ask how much the exam, urine test, blood tests, and medicine will cost. No matter how old your cat is, make sure that his urine is tested! Ask the veterinarian how the urine can be collected.

The veterinarian also may want to do a blood test, especially if the cat is older. This test will detect liver, kidney, or thyroid problems and will be useful as a baseline to evaluate changes in the cat's condition as time passes. Declawed cats should have their toes checked for infections or any other amputee-related problem.

If at all possible, avoid feeding dry food altogether when a litter box problem exists. If the veterinarian prescribes a specific dry food and it contains ethoxyquin, ask for alternatives. If feeding dry food is necessary, ask him about foods such Wysong Uretic or prescription foods, which are naturally preserved and are designed for urinary tract health.

If the veterinarian prescribes an antibiotic, steroid, antidepressant, or tranquilizer, find out what side effects and risks are associated with each medicine.

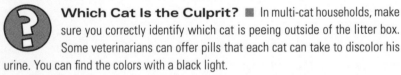

Which Cat Is the Culprit? ■ In multi-cat households, make sure you correctly identify which cat is peeing outside of the litter box. Some veterinarians can offer pills that each cat can take to discolor his urine. You can find the colors with a black light.

Most cats like to urinate when they first get up in the morning. Get up a little earlier some morning to spy on them.

Use a video camera to record events while you're not there. I know a cat owner who did that and discovered that a neighbor's cat was coming into the house through the cat door.

Handle with Care

If your cat urinates outside of the litter box, don't yell at him or rub his nose in the urine. Don't reprimand him. Don't show anger. Don't talk to your cat as if he is bad. But don't say his name or "poor baby" either. Just say "oh, no" or nothing at all. Act as though he's sick. Treating him as though he's bad will make matters worse.

Pick him up and take him to the litter box right away. Do not put him outside. Set up a confinement room with a litter box and a bowl of water, as described in Chapter 4, and lock him in.

In his confinement room, talk gently while showing him where things are. Have a wet meal ready and spend some time with him before he's left alone. Turn on a radio and a light. Keep the cat in the room whenever you can't watch him—even when you are on the phone or doing the dishes. It's best to keep him confined for two weeks. Being in a small room will force the cat to use his box.

Collecting Urine ■ If you think about collecting the urine yourself at home, be sure that the urine is fresh when tested. You must put it on ice right away and take it in immediately. Also, the urine sample must be clean. The cat needs to pee in a clean specimen cup, or in a clean empty box. Sometimes people will use Styrofoam packing material as a clean temporary "litter."

It's easier to have the veterinarian collect it to guarantee freshness.

Ask the veterinarian to squeeze the cat's bladder to collect urine rather than insert a catheter.

Neutralize the Urine

Because urine can permanently damage anything porous, thoroughly neutralize a urine spot on carpet or furniture. It's very important to not leave an odor that will attract a cat to pee there again.

If you're not sure exactly where the spot is, find it by feeling with a paper towel or by walking around in some old socks. Sniff the spot to make sure you found urine. It sounds gross, but if you don't get on your hands and knees to find it now, you won't have to get on your hands and knees to find it later—you'll just want to move away instead.

Commercial neutralizers are made especially for pet urine and are inexpensive, but vinegar also works as a stopgap measure. Buy the commercial stuff and apply it as soon as you can.

Sop up as much as you can with a sponge or paper towels. Apply the neutralizer according to the directions on the package. If your cat has peed on clothes or a pillow, wash the objects with some of the neutralizer and let them dry. You may want to inject neutralizer into the sofa, but test it for colorfastness first. Then cover the sofa and keep it covered until you know your cat's using his box again.

true story

One woman called me and was sure she needed to hire me. She was convinced that her cat was urinating outside the box because of the arrival of her new baby.

I told her I didn't think the cat's problem was behavioral. Most urine problems aren't. In most cases, the cat is either sick or stressed.

I was right. The owner called me up later and told me the cat almost died from a blockage in the bladder. The problem had been brewing for several months, but the owner mistook the cat's urination as a sign of behavioral problems.

If the urine has penetrated the carpet pad, try injecting neutralizer under the carpet with a syringe. If you have to replace the carpet, apply a special paint sealer to the floorboards. If the urine damage is deep enough, you may not get rid of the odor until you replace all affected floorboards and dry wall.

You must get rid of all un-neutralized urine spots in your house, even the old ones. A black light can help you find them. Shine the black light on carpet and walls to look for cat urine and cat spray. Also watch to see if your cat sniffs the floor or wall. It could be an old spot.

Keep all pets away from the spot until the urine has been totally neutralized. Cover it with a laundry basket or a piece of furniture to allow it to dry. When the spot is dry, guard it with rubber or a plastic carpet runner (either right side up or knobby side up).

Some neutralizers work right away, but some take two weeks. After removing the guard, place a food bowl or carpet runner on the spot to keep it inaccessible and to make him forget it was there. Don't use tinfoil to cover it up because the foil crumples and your cat could choke on it.

 Neutralizer Product List ■ These neutralizers are found at most pet stores, some hardware stores, and from mail order sources. Read the labels for instructions about how to use them. Many other products are on the market; only a few could be included here.

▶ Mother Nature's Odor Remover (powder and odor-removing bags), *www.mothernaturesodor.com*

▶ Get Serious! (stain, odor, and pheromone extractor), *www.getseriousproducts.com*.

▶ X-O Odor Neutralizer (natural and organic), *www.xocorp.com*.

▶ Especially for Cats Stain & Odor Remover, manufactured by Venus Pet Products, 1-800-592-1900

▶ Urine-Off, Odor & Stain Remover, *www.urine-off.com*

Improve His Litter Box Experience

Here are some tips for how to make sure your cat's litter box suits him well.

● Some cats won't go in the box because it's too dirty. Scoop solids and lift out wet spots daily. Keep the area around the box clean. Change the litter when it starts to smell, which is about once a week per cat. (See Chapter 7 for information about maintenance of litter boxes.)

● Make sure you have enough litter boxes. Set up one litter box per cat, plus one extra. If your home is too small for that many litter boxes, try to find a small litter box that fits snugly in a corner. These small triangular boxes are difficult to find but work surprisingly well for the small amount of room they take up. The corner boxes are very easy to clean and are a great way to add more litter boxes without taking up a lot of space.

- Put less litter in each box. Some cats will pee in a practically empty litter box.
- If he's using scented litter, try nonscented litter; if he's using clay litter, try pellets. Let your cat decide what he likes.

How Often Do I Need to Change the Litter? ▓ If you have one litter box per cat, as I recommend, you will probably need to change each box about once a week as well as scooping out the solids every day. If the cats use one box more than another, you'll need to change it more often. That means you can change the other one less often, so you still can average about once a week per box. Warning: If a box starts to smell, change it now. Read the cat litter package for instructions about minimizing the odor, too.

- Try different size litter boxes. Some cats like bigger boxes; some like smaller ones. Hardware and department stores stock utility boxes that are larger than the average litter boxes. Some stores carry smaller boxes, such as the corner litter box. Older cats or kittens may need a lower, shorter box.
- Try a covered litter box. Point the opening so your cat can see people or other pets approaching. Or, if you already have a covered box, try an uncovered one.
- Location is important. Unless your cat is very old or very young, keep the litter boxes away from their food, scratching posts, and beds. A bathroom or laundry room usually is a good place. Don't put it in a room he doesn't like to go in, or in an area that is heavily trafficked by dogs.
- Remove the plastic liner if you are using one. Some cats don't like the liner.
- Only touch a cat when he is inside the box if he raises his hind end to pee over the edge. Gently touch his rear end and hold it down. Don't say anything. Then buy a box with higher sides, or a covered box. Protect the floor and wall with plastic, or place the litter box inside a large television box with one side

and the top cut out. Drape newspapers over the edges; replace as needed. (See Chapter 7 for more information about litters, boxes, locations, and maintenance.)

Note: If the litter is kept clean, then the problem probably isn't the brand of litter. Something else is wrong when a cat stops using a well-maintained litter box.

Helpful Litter Box Hints ■ If your cat pees in a potted plant, cover the dirt with pinecones or decorative rocks.

If he pees on your bed, wash the bedding and neutralize mattress spots immediately. Later on, pet him or play with him on the bed.

Avoid putting a litter box directly on carpet, so that if he reaches outside the box to scratch at the litter, he doesn't snag the carpet. Protect your carpet with a runner, office mat, or plain cardboard.

More Help

Choose any ideas from this list that you think might help, considering your situation, time, patience, and budget.

- Stop feeding dry food, or stop leaving it out in between meals. If possible, feed only wet food, especially to old cats—they need all the moisture they can get. Add water to their wet food, too.
- Your cat may be allergic to some particular food or ingredient. Try more chicken- and lamb-based foods, fresh meat or fish, and vegetables, as well as whole grains.
- Withhold food products and supplements containing yeast for a month, or until the urination problem is under control. Slowly add the yeast product back into his diet. If a reaction occurs, he could be sensitive to some products containing yeast.
- Don't feed salt or salty foods, which will make him drink more water. Salt can strain already weary kidneys; besides, cats weren't designed to drink a lot of water.

- Add fiber to his diet, and try a hairball remedy (see Chapter 14).
- Feed him roasted chicken necks twice a week. They have a lot of calcium.
- If you're desperate, stop feeding canned food altogether and feed only raw organic foods.

 Did You Know? ■ A cat in the wild is more meticulous about covering up his waste the closer he is to his nest.

- An old cat may not be able to wait to be let outside or to make it down to the basement in the middle of the night. Put a litter box on each level of the house and near the room where he sleeps. Also keep a litter box on each level for a kitten until it is old enough to know its way around the house.
- Make sure you have a litter box indoors even if your cat is allowed outside. He needs a place that is always safe.
- Too many pets in too little space causes stress. Adding an outdoor kennel could provide some additional space and stress relief, especially if the kennel is accessible from indoors. (See Chapter 19 for more information.)
- If your cat is frightened by constant or frequent noise and commotion, try to set up a quiet place for him to retreat to. An open carrier case with a blanket in it is good. Playing music can help cover the noise of nearby construction or traffic.
- Don't leave dirty clothes or bad-smelling articles such as shoes lying about. Some cats will pee on rank-smelling stuff.
- Speak to other members of the household. Make sure everyone understands how to treat the cat. Ask them to help you with feeding the cat and cleaning up after it.
- Being an only cat may be difficult for many cats. But don't get a new cat until the litter box problem is solved.
- Some cats only pee outside the box when their owners come home from vacation. Just in case, pay special attention to your

cat when you get home. Before you look at the mail or listen to phone messages, spend time with him. Play with him. As soon as he uses his box, go to the kitchen and feed him a wet meal. If you will be gone for more than two days, get someone to visit your cat at least once a day.

- Eastern medicine hands-on remedies like Jin Shin Jyutsu, Reiki, or Tellington Touch may help. You can take lessons in using these techniques so you can help your cat yourself.

- Contact a cat behaviorist for advice. Ask questions to assure yourself that she or he is qualified. A few behaviorists are listed in the Products and Resources section of the Appendix. Many animal shelters can direct you to free help, or refer you to someone who knows about cat behavior problems.

- A cat door could be letting strange cats inside the house. Your cat may be intimidated by the intruder and use peeing as a way to mark his territory. The strange cat might even be the one doing the peeing. To make sure that can't happen, close off pet doors while you're not home. This can help reduce the stress your cat may have if he's intimidated by intruders.

 WARNING ▪ Do not put compost containing cat waste on the garden. Cat waste is not suitable compost material.

- Ultrasound or x-rays may find kidney stones that a urine test could miss. Call around for price quotes, because this can be expensive.

- If these measures don't work, your cat may need the additional help for declawed cats described in the next section.

Special Considerations

Special considerations are made for declawed cats because they are most likely to have litter box problems. (Declawing is an amputation of toes on an animal that uses his feet to cover it's waste.) These tips can also help emotionally or physically challenged cats that need special attention:

Declawing a cat makes him "litter-boxed challenged." Because declawed cats have a lower tolerance for stress and a higher risk of pain, their litter box problems frequently are more difficult to solve. Even years after the operation, the declawed cat can easily lose bathroom manners when he becomes upset—and often, it doesn't take much to upset him.

true story

I knew a double-declawed cat that was kept on a six-foot chain next to his bed, litter box, and food for almost ten years. And he wasn't neutered because he "wasn't let outside." Thank goodness that cat is no longer alive. This was not a good last resort.

To minimize the declawed cat's stress levels:

- Give him *daily, supervised* time outdoors. This often relieves his problems for a while.
- Massage him and give him positive attention often.
- Make sure his meals and outdoor times are on a reliable, daily schedule. It's important to minimize changes in routine for a cat that is disabled or may suffer from pain.
- Supplement his diet with vitamins that can help him deal with stress. Vitamins such as B-complex, C (ascorbic acid), and vitamin E every day or every other day may help. Squeeze 100-IU vitamin E from a gel cap (made for people or cats) and add a pinch of vitamin C (ascorbic acid powder or crystals) onto his wet food. Some cats may eat the vitamin E gel straight from a punctured capsule. Anitra Frazier's book *The New Natural Cat* has additional specifics for using vitamins.
- One easy way to give vitamins is to buy multiple vitamins that

are specially prepared for pets. Many kinds are sold in health food stores. Tasha's Herbs for Cats is one that comes in a variety of formulas. Use the drops as directed, and check the expiration date before buying or using them. Avoid products that contain sugar.

- Give him fresh, organic catnip once or twice a week.
- Bad weather and changes in the barometer can affect joints and bones and cause pain in your declawed cat's toes, which may in turn lead to litter box problems. On days when your declawed cat seems especially moody, give him chicken broth with a pinch of ascorbic acid (get powder or crystals at a health food store). Put four drops of Bach Flower Rescue Remedy in fresh drinking water. Massages can do wonders on those days. Catnip, too.
- Play peaceful music. Leave a radio on low volume to drown out any distressing noises.
- Put a night-light by his litter box.
- When moving to a new house, be especially gentle and conscious of his needs during and after the move. Be slow about letting the declawed cat get full use of the house. (See Chapter 6, Change Happens for more information.)
- Store things like laundry, quilts, crocheted afghans, and yarn away from your cat. All of these may be tempting places to pee for a cat with sore paws.

Litter Box Considerations for Declawed Cats

- Spoon out solids and wet urine spots as often as possible.
- Find out which litter he likes best by trying two or three different litters at a time. Disposable litter boxes or cardboard boxes of litter box size can help with the test. Each week keep one of the brands that he likes, but fill the other boxes with other

litter brands. Keep in mind that while clawed cats rarely quit using their customary litter unless something is wrong, declawed cats are more finicky. Sometimes changing the litter will work for a while, but does not address the underlying causes of the litter box problem. Still, it's a worth a try.

- If clay litters haven't worked, try soft litters such as SWHEAT, Here's the Scoop! or World's Best Cat Litter. These are biodegradable clumping litters that do not contain sodium bentonite.

- If you're using nonclumping litter, try half the amount you've been using. Shake the litter to one end so only half of the floor is covered. Each time you remove the solids, shake to expose half of the floor again. He may prefer to step onto a smooth plastic floor.

- Avoid relocating a litter box. If you have to, get a new litter box and set it up in the new location. After he's gotten used to its being there, remove the old one.

Shopping List for Declawed Cats with Litter Box Problems

- ✓ catnip
- ✓ different litter brands
- ✓ Bach Flower Rescue Remedy or flower essence remedy to relieve pain and stress
- ✓ Tasha's Herbs for Cats
- ✓ foods and supplements for stress and immune system (containing vitamins C, E, and B-complex)
- ✓ ascorbic acid (vitamin C) powder or crystals
- ✓ low sodium chicken broth
- ✓ night-light or light timer
- ✓ Kitty Korner Komber Self-Grooming Aid for CATS
- ✓ underpads (see Litter Alternatives section of this chapter)

Litter Alternatives

If you've tried many types of litter and your declawed cat doesn't like any of them, here are some alternatives.

Grass clippings. Grass clippings neutralize urine well and are soft. Leave the clippings outside for a few days to let them dry. Protect the floor surrounding the litter box with plain cardboard to avoid grass stains. Monitor the box and remove solids daily. Dump and wash it and add fresh grass as needed. Don't use grass treated with a pesticide or weed killer.

Newspaper and paper towels. Line a litter box with a few sheets of newspaper, covered with paper towels. To let cats know it's the litter box, spoon some soiled litter on top of the paper towel. Change the papers after every use.

Potting soil. Try using all potting soil, or mix some with a non-clumping litter. Gradually keep using more litter and less soil.

Underpads. These are 23" × 36" disposable, flat diapers, often used in nursing homes. These pads provide a steady, absorbent alternative to cat litter. Sprinkle a little of Mother Nature's Odor Remover on the pad to control the odor and add a spoonful of cat litter to let him know it's a litter box. I buy these underpads from Target, and I cut them in half to line a litter box. These also can be taped to a wall where a cat might be spraying.

 Helpful Hint ■ If your cat is declawed, put a litter box in the bathtub. Many declawed cats would rather scratch at the side of the litter box than on rough litter. Be sure to protect the drain from litter and dust.

Last Resorts

If your cat is not declawed and he's not white, you could keep him outside during the day. (White cats are easily sunburned.) Being outside and unsupervised is less safe but has worked as a last resort for many cat owners. If you must keep him outside, try to make your yard as safe as possible by finding a way to keep him inside of it, such as by installing a cat kennel or special guards on top of your fence. You usually can find these guards advertised in the back of cat magazines. Because he's more at risk from animals and other dangers at night, bring him indoors and keep him in a confinement room before it gets dark.

One last resort I do not recommend is locking a cat in one room for the rest of its life. Many people tell me "the cat lives in the basement now." This is no way to live with a cat. And it's no way for a cat to live.

true story

Owners of declawed cats tell me they maintain the litter box daily. They've tried all different types of litter. A typical complaint from them is that "sometimes he'll be fine for a few weeks, then he'll start up again. . ."

Sometimes nothing works. A cat that continues to pee outside the litter box probably is suffering. Cats are very, very clean animals—it's unnatural for healthy cats to spoil their living area and urinate outside the litter box. In most cases, I have found that cats that repeatedly urinate outside the litter box are sick, in pain, feral, abused, and/or suffering a physical disability such as missing a limb or being declawed. Most often, declawed cats are the ones that continue no matter how many solutions you try. Although no one likes to bring it up, some cat owners have had no option other than putting a declawed cat to sleep. His litter box problem is not likely to get better in a different home with a different family, and it's too cruel and dangerous to keep him outside. This decision never is reached lightly. You must keep in mind that an unchecked urine problem poses a health hazard and can end up costing you a lot of money in home repairs. When suffering is suspected, euthanasia is the most humane alternative.

Just remember—happy, healthy cats don't pee outside the litter box. Your next cat, if he keeps his claws, has an excellent chance of having good litter box habits for his entire life.

Miscellaneous Problems

Does your cat wake you earlier than you want in the morning? Does he accidentally snag his claws in your clothes? Is he timid? This chapter covers these and other common complaints that cat owners have.

The Early Morning Cat

A cat that runs across your bed, scratches at your blankets, and purrs in your face before you want to get up in the morning is annoying. The problem gets worse when the owner waits before giving in to the cat. The cat learns to be obnoxious longer the next morning until the owner gives in again. Pretty soon, the owner is getting up at 3:00 A.M. or 4:00 A.M. The trick is to not give him what he wants when he asks you for something while you're sleeping:

Here are some other things you can do:

- Provide an indoor litter box so he won't pester you to let him outside when he wakes up too early.
- If he's allowed outside, let him out at a regular time every day. Don't let him out at any other time of the day. Don't let a cat outside right after you get out of bed. He will learn that bugging you while you're still in bed will not get him what he wants.

Shopping List

Morning Cats

✓ perfume
✓ carpet runner
✓ cat toys

Velvet Paws; Curtain and Screen Climbing

✓ nail trimmers
✓ nylon netting

Spraying

✓ urine neutralizer
✓ carpet cleaner
✓ carpet runner
✓ organic catnip
✓ vitamins
✓ bare wooden post, tree limb, or cardboard scratching pad

Shy Cats

✓ cat treats
✓ cat toys

Chewers

✓ fiber supplements
✓ catnip spray
✓ chew toys, graphite pencils, yardsticks

See the Products and Resources section in the Appendix for more information.

- Serve him his meals at regular times each day. Do not feed him as soon as you get out of bed. Take your shower and get your tea ready before giving him his morning meal. He'll get used to it.
- If the cat likes to cuddle up to your head or neck but you'd rather have him by your feet, gently move him down the bed and pet him. If he moves back up, keep moving him down until he gets tired. Some cats don't like perfume or cologne; spray some on your neck before going to bed.
- Scare him when he hassles you while you're in bed. When he runs across you, lift your knee in front of him and yell "No." Gently shove him off the bed. If a cat is really bugging me, I sometimes violate my own advice about never holding the cat against his will and will hold and hug him to make it difficult

for him to leave. Because cats don't like to be held down, this may curb the behavior faster.

- Protect the carpet outside of your bedroom door by covering it with something sturdy, such as a carpet runner. Cut the carpet runner to match the width of the doorway. As soon as your cat turns obnoxious, shut him out of the room. The cat won't be happy about being locked out. He will do his best to wear you down. He'll scratch at the carpet runner near the door to be let in. Don't give in! If you let him in, he'll be more persistent the next day. If you really have to open your door to make him stop, do not talk to him. Just pick him up and lock him in a room that has a litter box and water, and go back to bed.

true story

One of my clients adopted a cat that had been kept in an animal shelter for nine months. To quiet this early morning cat, my client set up a large cage with a small litter box, a bed, and water. His cat walked into the cage on his own and slept soundly all night with the cage door open.

- Put a scratching post right outside your bedroom door so he'll have a way to vent frustration at not being let in.
- Put toys in other rooms so he can play while you sleep.
- Put a cat bed by a window, and a bird feeder just outside for him to watch. This helps keep him occupied in the twilight hours, when he's most likely to be active.
- Playing with your cat for several minutes, once or twice a day, helps tire him for the night.

Velvet Paws

Some cats are sloppy about keeping their claws retracted and will accidentally snag your clothes and furniture and scratch your skin. Teaching a cat to have "velvet paws" means to train the cat to not extend the claws. It also means teaching the owner how to handle the cat so he's never forced to use his claws.

Before beginning, your cat should be used to having his claws trimmed. (See the Chapter 14.)

Here is the essence of velvet paw training: Never let him hurt you. When he does scratch you or snag something, say "Ouch!" and trim one or two of his claws. The key to success is to react immediately. Sharply say "Ouch!" the instant it happens, even if he snags the clothes you're wearing. Then look at his nails and say, "You need your nails trimmed." Trim one or two claws while talking to him in a gentle tone. Then pull out a lure toy to make him forget about his nail trim, or pet him and tell him he's a good boy. If trying to trim a nail causes fear or panic in your cat, then wait until he is asleep.

true story

I started velvet paw training with Louie when he was three weeks old. By eight weeks he was the most gentle little guy. Now, even as a large adult, when he "kneads" my face, his claws won't hurt me.

Tips for Preventing Scratches

If your cat is frightened while you are holding him, he may extend his claws and try to jump down. Even after he is velvet pawed, he may dig his claws into you when he's suddenly frightened. It's important when holding a cat to always hold him in a such a way and release him in such a way that you avoid his claws touching you. Be ready, willing, and able to let him go at any time. Don't hold him in a way that would cause him to hurt you should he scramble to get away. And never hold him close to your face, because you are unprotected should he bolt.

While he's learning, avoid handling him while you're wearing delicate clothing. If he tends to scratch you accidentally, wear long sleeves and handle him very carefully until he's used to keeping his claws in. If your cat's claws are trimmed properly, accidental scratching usually will not break the skin.

Keep your cat's claws trimmed short all the time. This, in itself, will prevent most accidental snagging. Even the best cat can't prevent a sharp point from catching material and hurting your skin.

Helpful Hint ▪ To give kittens and cats some fun, drape an old sheet over a piece of furniture so that it nearly touches the floor. Spray it once with catnip so they knows it's an okay place to hide and play. Cats will play with each other on opposite sides of the drape.

Curtain and Screen Climbing

Kittens will sometimes climb curtains. Adult cats usually are too heavy for curtains but can rip window screens. It's best to stop this behavior as soon as it starts and then begin teaching your cat good window habits.

Protect your curtains by pinning them up out of the way whenever a kitten is loose. If he tries to jump on the curtains, say "no" immediately and carry him to the scratching post.

If your cat scratches a window screen, spend a few minutes a day with him when the window is open and the screen is exposed. Whenever a claw goes into the screen, deliver a firm "No!" and clip a nail. If he does it again, clip another nail. If he does it a third time, shut the window. Until he stops damaging the screen, keep your windows closed when you aren't around, or cover the open window with nylon netting.

Spraying

When a cat sprays, he's marking territory with a horizontal stream of urine. He stands high up on all fours and aims at the wall. This problem is different from urinating outside the box. Spraying is considered a behavior problem, whereas a urine problem is often a sign of illness. I consider spraying a sign of aggression, low self-esteem, or stress, all of which can be helped by diet and exercise. If the problem is not solved, his spray could destroy your house.

Causes and Cures

If you catch him spraying, firmly tell him "No." Carry him to a room that has a litter box and lock him in. Clean and neutralize the soiled area before letting your cat out. If you can, wash the area again while your cat watches. This shows him that the walls are yours, not his.

Tape underpads on the walls where he has sprayed. Also protect the floor next to the wall with underpads and plastic carpet runner. (See the Litter Alternatives section of Chapter 21.)

If you haven't already done so, spay or neuter your cat. This alleviates most spraying problems. (Note that I used the word "most." The urine is less potent and the behavior is less likely in neutered cats, but some fixed cats do spray.)

Living in overcrowded situations can cause stress, frustration, and anger, which in turn can lead to spraying. The cat may spray to protect the little territory that he feels he owns. You can alleviate overcrowding by taking some cats outside regularly. (See Chapter 19 for ways to take cats outside safely.) Make sure that you play with him and that he uses the scratching post every day. A bare wooden post or tree limb for him to scratch may help to relieve your cat's stress. The bare wood simulates a natural place for his paws to leave his scent. Provide healthful diet and exercise. (See Chapter 12 for more about diet and Chapter 11 for exercise guidelines.) Give him vitamins and catnip to help ease stress. (See Chapter 21.)

If your cat lives indoors only, confine him to one room for a week or two. Then gradually let him have use of the rest of the house again. (See Chapter 4 for more about confinement.) If he usually goes outside, let him outdoors only at the regular time. Wait at least an hour if he was due to go out soon after a spraying incident. If he has no regular outdoor time, don't let him outside until the next day. If the problem persists, confine him in a room for a week or two. This helps limit the territory he feels he must protect. When he is out of confinement and into the rest of the house again, see if his spraying has stopped. If it has, you may try outside walks again, but only if you can stick with a consistent, daily schedule.

true story

Sam was two years old when I adopted him. He used to raise havoc in the apartment—before I had him neutered. Some nights he'd pull out the drawer of the bird cage so he could stick his front leg into the cage and frighten the parakeets. Other nights he would paw the kitchen cabinets and rattle around in the pots and pans. Then, about a month after I adopted Sam, I saw him back up to the wall and shoot a stream of urine.

I called the veterinarian for an appointment to neuter him. Sam never sprayed inside the house again. He even stopped rattling the pots and pans around in the kitchen at night. We found another home for the birds.

Sometimes a cat sprays after seeing or even hearing a strange cat outside the house. Keeping a scratching post near the windows or doors can help your cat relieve frustration or anger. If your cat gets upset by a strange cat, distract him with a lure toy or a food treat *before* he sprays. Using his name, say things like "You are so brave!" He'll probably cool down and forget about being angry.

Keep a cat bed by the window so that he can watch and protect the house even while he naps. He may feel less threatened if he can see outside. I don't believe that covering the windows is a good idea. You can't hide something from an animal whose hearing and smelling capabilities are even better than his eyesight. And besides, covered windows are no way for people to live.

Provide a low, horizontal scratching board. Scratching horizontally is another way that a cat will mark territory.

If you've tried everything and he still sprays, ask your veterinarian to check for impacted anal glands, and for medication that may alleviate the problem.

Some cats truly aren't meant to stay indoors and may benefit from temporary use of tranquilizers. Letting the cat stay outside may be the best alternative. See the Last Resorts section of Chapter 21.

Shy Cats

Does your cat run away when other people or cats are around? Is he too easily frightened by everyday events? Although cats have a tendency to run away first before approaching something new, eventually his curiosity should win out. Some cats will hide for a couple of days after a move; other than that, not many cats hide every day unless something is wrong.

The stress of being on the streets and in the shelter can cause some adopted cats to go into "shell shock," which forces them to hide. Being around dogs may cause your cat to hide a lot too, but he could be sick, so take him to the veterinarian to be sure. Being handicapped is another possible cause of shyness. A shy cat also may not have been handled much, or may have been mishandled, mistreated, abused, ignored, and rarely praised or petted, especially when young. It has been proven that proper handling of kittens leads to healthier adult cats.

What Else to Do?

Gradually accustom your cat to handling and massages. Be sure to stop *before* he gets nervous. (For tips on technique, see Chapter 13.) Say your cat's name and talk to him gently whenever he comes around, or even when he just looks in the doorway. Train your cat to come when called. This helps to build trust. (See Chapter 18 to learn how to do this training.) Play with your cat daily, one-on-one, in a bedroom with the door closed. Use lure toys or string, and let him catch the toy often. One or two fifteen-minute sessions each day should help increase your cat's confidence and help him overcome shyness. Don't use large feathers as a toy, because they may be intimidating for an already timid cat. And remember to always store string or lure toys away from your cat when you aren't around.

true story
Louie comes and tells me when he wants certain things. Throughout the day, he'll ask me for playing, food, massages, or outside. I give him what he wants only if it's about the usual time he normally gets them. By knowing he can depend on routine, he cries a lot less. On the occasions when I cannot give him what he wants, I tell him "Not now" and he gives up on it.

Encourage him to use the scratching post more. Strong muscles build confidence. (See Chapter 11 for ways to do this.)

If he doesn't like being held, avoid picking him up. Pet him where he's standing or lying down. If you want to hold him, get down on his level and gently walk him into your lap to avoid picking him up. He'll be more likely to start approaching you on his own that way. If your friends are visiting, warn them not to pick up the shy cat. Ask them to not say his name or "it's okay" if your cat runs away or acts scared. Just ignore him unless he approaches you or your friends. Then talk to him gently or get out a lure toy and play with him.

Provide him with elevated hiding places or a special cat bed. Cats like to view the world from a high vantage point. Looking down at the family can build trust.

If he's extremely timid, set up a confinement room as described in Chapter 4. A big house is overwhelming for a really scared guy. Keep him in his nursery for one to three weeks. Feed and visit him regularly. Use treats to entice him into having contact with you. Each day, spend as much time in the nursery as you can, playing with him, massaging him, and being with him. The more he responds to your touch, coming toward you and coming to your call, the more freedom he can be allowed.

I do one thing to a shy cat that I don't otherwise do: If I know it's a time when he won't hurt me, I hold him against his will for a brief second or two—long enough to pet him using a forceful yet compassionate stroke, but not so long that he gets really fussy. Sometimes just a little loving hug can make some cats who were thinking of getting away decide to hang out for a few more seconds. Also, it's best to settle him down for a second or two before letting him go, so he's likely to hang around longer next time. Don't wait until he's antsy to let a shy cat go.

Crying Cats

When your cat cries, he's usually trying to tell you something. Find out what he wants. Does he want to go outside, or eat, or play? Or is he maybe sick, lonely, or frightened? Or is he just the sort of cat that naturally whines a lot?

- If your cat cries while using the litter box, call the veterinarian immediately.
- Sticking to his daily routine of play, meals, and outdoor times helps avoid whining. Play with him at least twice a day.
- Using his name, ask him, "What do you want, Louie?" and follow him to where he walks. A cat will walk to his eating, outside, or play area. If it's not the right time to eat or go outside or you can't play right now, tell him "Not now." Do *not* give in! Direct a clawed cat to the scratching post. By the time he's done, he won't remember what he was whining about. If later you want to take him outside or give him his special treat, wait until he's sleeping and then call "Here," using his name.
- If he doesn't lead you anywhere, he may just want lots of loving from you—that is, petting and massage. Or he may be frightened

or not feeling well. Pet him and comfort him. Put a night-light on where he sleeps at night. Keep an eye on him and take him to the veterinarian if he shows any symptoms of illness or injury.

 WARNING ■ Cover electrical cords with plastic safety coverings from a hardware store. A spray-on repellent may not be enough to stop your cat from chewing.

- If he cries to you for something that he is scheduled to get at that time, give it to him as soon as he asks for it. Don't let him cry for half an hour if he's asking for something at the proper time.
- Make sure the cat gets attention during the times when he's quiet and good.
- If these measures don't work, your cat simply could be a natural-born whiner, like Louie. He has been since week one.

Chewers

Although it is relatively rare, cats sometimes develop destructive chewing habits. You may find your cat chewing on objects such as furniture, electrical cords, or shoes. This behavior may be caused by stress, boredom, or a nutritional deficiency.

Because each cat is different, use your instinct to decide what might be causing the problem. In any case, secure your house by covering the electrical cords, putting your shoes away, and protecting other things that he's likely to chew. Put perfume on objects that you don't want him to chew, so that he will know they are your property. Spray catnip on the things that he's allowed to chew, so he'll know what stuff belongs to him.

Here, Chew on This!

Set up things around the house that he is allowed to chew on, such as the following:

- A yardstick or small branch tucked under a sofa cushion, where it will be steady while he chews on it
- A dog chew toy or a large soup bone, left in a place where he likes to chew
- A cardboard box (open the top flap of the box to about your cat's height so he can chew on it)
- Unsharpened graphite pencils

When you catch him chewing on things he shouldn't, tell him "not here" and direct him to something he can chew. If it's there, he'll go to it. Even then, rather than set up your cat for failure—and yourself for disappointment—don't leave your fancy shoes out. When you leave the house, cover up valuable things he's likely to chew. Keep the electrical cords covered. Go back to whatever he was chewing on and protect it or put it away.

Once you think you know what caused the chewing problem, customize your approach as follows:

- To minimize stress, establish an exercise regimen as outlined in Chapters 11 and 21. Play with him regularly, and supplement his diet with vitamins C, E, and B-complex to lessen stress.
- If he's alone for extended periods of time, he may be bored. Consider getting another cat for him to play with. If that's not realistic, see Owning an Only Cat in Chapter 3 for suggestions. In addition, increase your time with him.
- He may be chewing household objects because he's not getting enough fiber. Add pet fiber supplement, cooked brown rice, and/or catnip to his diet. Some fiber supplements are made specifically for cats. (See Products and Resources in the Appendix.)

Part 4
Aging

193   23 ● Growing Old and Saying Goodbye

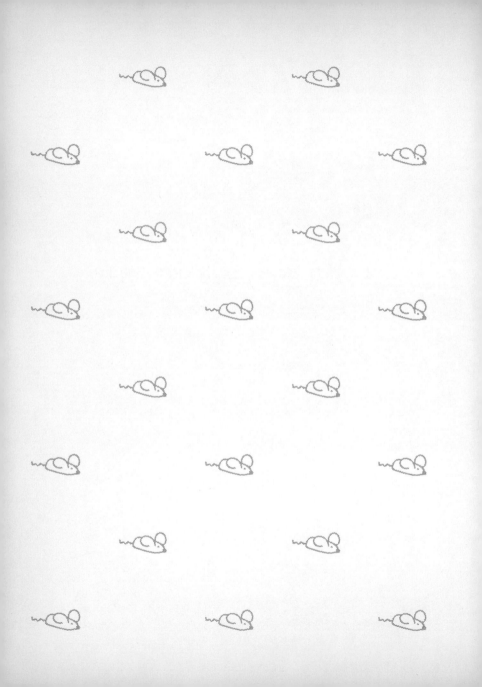

23

Growing Old and Saying Goodbye

🐾 Time passes very quickly when we own cats. All too soon it will be time to say goodbye. Cats live to be about fifteen to twenty years old, and I keep hearing about cats that are even older than that. Aging brings on problems in cats that are similar to those of aging people, such as stiff joints and failing eyesight and hearing.

Signs of aging include reduced mobility, diminished appetite and corresponding weight loss, and occasional incontinence. When you first notice one of these symptoms, ask the veterinarian to give your cat a physical and a blood test.

As your cat ages and has trouble getting around, there are several things you can do.

● Unless otherwise instructed by your veterinarian, feed an older cat five or six very small wet meals a

Shopping List

✔ floor-level, warm bed
✔ extra litter box
✔ whatever she will eat
✔ special treats, such as tuna and baby food (chicken, beef, turkey)
✔ blanket or towel

Optional

✔ burial basket or box
✔ grave marker

See the Products and Resources section in the Appendix for more information.

193

day so she doesn't have to process so much food at once. Stop using low-fat or "senior" food—you now need to help your cat fight the tendency to lose weight. Don't feed her dry food any more, because it strains the kidneys, which often are the first major organs to quit.

- To keep her fit, keep encouraging her to use the scratching post. Have one by her bed. You also should take her on short walks outside. But remember that she isn't good at protecting herself now, so be sure to supervise her at all times.

- Keep a litter box and water bowl on each level in your home. Asking an elderly cat to climb stairs (and relatively tall stairs at that) to relieve herself is unreasonable. Make toilet provisions on every level for a cat that has trouble getting around.

 Cats Are Like People ■ When we get old, everything we do is more of a challenge.

- Brush and massage your senior cat often. Elderly cats aren't able to groom themselves as they once used to, and they will appreciate a tender, loving touch.

- Have a night-light so your cat can find her litter box more easily at night.

- Put a warm, draft-free bed at floor level so she doesn't have to climb or jump to take her nap.

- Gently massage, or simply hold, her frail body whenever you have the time.

A Cat's Final Days

When your cat's appetite and bladder control are completely gone, her breathing is difficult, or she drinks constantly, she may be near the end. Check with the veterinarian. At this point, give your cat whatever she wants—even "no-no" foods such as tuna or baby food.

As the end nears, you will need to make some horrible decisions. Dying at home in "her own time" is often not without suffering. You may want to consider euthanasia. It's a difficult decision to let go, but sometimes it's more humane to have a compassionate veterinarian gently put her to sleep.

If you decide to have her put to sleep, make arrangements with the veterinarian. Many veterinarians will come to your house, or you can take your cat to the vet's office. While you're on the phone, discuss with the doctor what to do with the body. You can bury it, arrange to have it cremated, or let the veterinarian take care of the remains. Ask any questions now, especially delicate ones, because you won't be in the mood to ask about them later.

When it's time to go, take a blanket or towel with you so your cat can die on a soft bed rather than a hard table. Have someone else drive so that you can hold your cat in your lap. She'll be so sick by that time that she won't need a carrier unless you are driving alone. I recommend having someone else drive so that you won't have to drive home by yourself.

The veterinarian will ask you to sign a release form before starting. Ask him to not scruff your cat at any time. Let your cat's last moments be as dignified as possible. Put the blanket under your cat on the table and spend some tender moments with her while the first shot, a sedative, is taking effect.

When you are ready to have your cat put to sleep, the veterinarian might need to shave the cat's leg so that he or she can see the correct vein in which to make the injection. It's okay if you leave before the vet administers the actual euthanasia shot, and it's also okay if you stay. It won't be easy either way. Go with whatever you think you can handle. If you do leave, don't feel guilty later for not "being there"—your cat knows you love her.

Handling the Grief

It's normal and perfectly all right to grieve the loss of your cat. Take all the time you need. It's very difficult to lose a companion that you loved and lived with, even if that companion was not a human being. Many people don't realize how sad they feel until the cat is truly gone. Don't feel too bad when others don't understand your grief—to many people, she was "just a cat." If you are easily hurt by a lack of compassion, tell people that you lost a "close friend of the family" and leave it at that.

 Buyer's Remorse ■ Don't adopt a new cat just because she looks like your old cat did—there is no way she'll be like your old cat. Each cat is different. Look at her behavior, not her looks. Read Chapter 3 for more guidance.

It's very easy to bring home the wrong cat shortly after losing one. To help avoid this, volunteer with your local shelter to foster cats for a few months. If you're unsure about what kind of cats to foster, ask someone at the shelter about black cats. Then adopt the cat you love to live with!

Some cat owners hold a memorial ceremony to help deal with the loss and establish closure. Some write goodbye letters and bury the letters with the cat's remains, along with a favorite toy. Others add a grave marker to identify the grave. Do whatever seems right to you.

Your local shelter may offer a support group where you can talk about your loss. You also may want to take anti-stress vitamins, get some exercise, relax in soothing hot baths, and eat as healthfully as possible so you don't react to your cat's death by getting sick.

true story
Our Sam had about a week left after he was diagnosed with a kidney problem. Every day of that week, I took him into the yard and spent hours watching him while he enjoyed his favorite places and did his favorite things: talking to birds, dozing off, smelling plants, enjoying the sun, making believe he was a great

hunter. I took time to comfort Sam with my hands and told him about how we met and our years together. . . about how much I appreciated his company, how much I loved him, and how he was there for me through hard times. I thanked him for sharing his life with me.

Three days before he died, he stopped eating and began drinking a lot of water. His kidneys were shutting down.

It's a difficult thing to plan your own cat's death. But my husband made it easier when he said that he did not want Sam to have any bad days. I realized I felt the same way. The next morning we took Sam into the backyard for a last visit. Then, all too soon, after fourteen years of loving and living with Sam, it was time to let him go.

When the veterinarian told us he would shave Sam's inner thigh and inject the lethal shot there, I ran crying from the room—I couldn't watch him die.

Sam died in his "father's" arms. It was very quick, and then Sam was gone. Afterward, Bruce came out into the waiting room and cried with me.

We had Sam cremated. When we got his ashes back, we held a ceremony with candles, a song, and eulogies, and then we buried his ashes in a small wicker basket. He rests now in his favorite "rolling around" place, at the base of a pine tree.

When the time is right, think about getting another cat. It is very healing to have another cat to care for and love. Although many people may think they are paying tribute to old "Simon" by waiting to adopt, what about the new "Fred" that's waiting at the shelter for you today? He could be ashes by tomorrow. *Cats need you.* Give another cat a chance to live in your home and experience your love and care.

Appendix

201   Declawing Drawbacks

214   Cute Cat Tricks

217   Cat Maintenance Schedule

220   Cat Advocacy

228   Donations Needed

231   Products and Resources

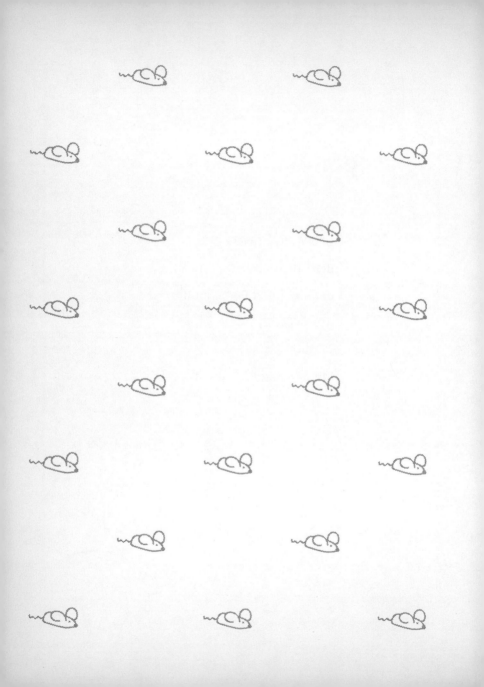

I wouldn't declaw a
cat if you paid me
$1,000 per nail!

Dr. Louis J. Camuti, DVM

Declawing Drawbacks

Declawing is presented to cat owners as a rational choice, yet it creates often insurmountable problems for both the cat and its owner. Owning a declawed cat is neither cheap nor easy. A cat needs his claws to groom, scratch, climb, exercise, "knead," and to rake cat litter in comfort. Adopting a declawed cat is different from adopting one that has all his "fingers." Don't expect him to be the same, feel the same, act the same, cost the same, or be as healthy as able-bodied cats.

It should come as no surprise that declawing immediately jeopardizes a cat's entire life in many, many ways. Besides challenging the physical and mental capabilities of the cat, it challenges those of an owner who was not warned of the drawbacks of declawing.

We choose declawing because we've been convinced that it will solve a problem. In fact, declawing causes many more problems than it solves. Peeing outside the box is just one, and it's enough in and of itself. Cat urine can destroy your home much faster and more thoroughly than claws ever would.

When owners of declawed cats call me, it's almost always about litter box problems. "I did what my vet said. . . our home is still being destroyed by cat urine. . . we've replaced the carpet. . . we threw out the sofa. . . we clean the litter daily. . . and he still pees. . . I'm thinking of getting rid of him."

Dealing with the urine problems of a cat that cannot learn to use a litter box requires the patience of a saint. And few of us, when it comes down to it, are saints. How would you feel if your couch was totally ruined by urine? Or if your carpet, pad, and floorboards stank to the point that they had to be replaced? I know owners of declawed cats who have had to do this. People who own clawed cats rarely call me about damage as extensive as this.

Many people simply can't and won't face the stench of urine, and not many cat owners will let a cat destroy an entire house. In desperation, they may try to force him to live outside. When he's outside, he is an easy target for predators.

Cats Are Like People ■ You don't have to declaw a cat just because all of your other cats are declawed. Cats, like people, recognize another's handicap immediately. It's perfectly okay to mix clawed and declawed cats inside the house.

Some argue that removing the front claws is of no consequence because a cat fights primarily with his hind paws. This is not the whole truth: A cat *escapes* by climbing trees with his front claws. Which would be better—a cat that has defenses only to fight, or one that also can get away? Too many declawed cats are rushed to emergency rooms after trying to get away from dogs. Contrary to myth, most cats don't like to fight. Cats would rather escape.

If making the cat live outside stops "working," and if the cat continues to pee inside the house, the cat will be given new "last resorts." Owners will start to use alternatives that the veterinarian didn't mention at the time of declawing. The owners may squirt or spank the cat, or imprison him in one room or in the basement. They may give away or abandon the cat, not knowing that declawing was what started their mess. Others will have the cat destroyed. Many cat owners are unconsciously made aware that declawing is nowhere near the "last resort." Death is.

Even if the cat is allowed to stay indoors, he won't have much of a life. He'll be clumsy, more prone to infections, more moody, and more trouble than a clawed cat. And he won't be able to exercise and use carpeted cat trees the way clawed cats do.

Cats and dogs exercise in very different ways: Cats stalk, dogs hunt. Cats evolved to sleep and scratch, not run and pant. It's very difficult to get a cat to run at all, let alone on sore feet. Some declawed cats have sore feet their entire lives (not just the two weeks some veterinarians may claim). And every cat scratches, whether his mother taught him when he was born or not. Declawing does not change a cat's internal need to do this. It does, however, make it more painful and challenging.

Did You Know? ■ The declawing procedure involves anesthesia and cutting off the cat's toes to the first knuckle. Many veterinarians use a tool similar to pruning shears. Others use a "fine scalpel" technique, or laser. They claim these are cleaner procedures—which they probably are—but no matter how you cut it, declawing is crippling the cat.

The operation takes about 10 minutes and can cost anywhere from $50 to $450. But the costs and pain don't stop there. For some cats and owners, the problems are just beginning. If the cat comes down with an infection or develops behavioral problems as a result of declawing, the follow-up care and repairs can be very expensive.

Mayo Clinic Family Health Book author and editor-in-chief David E. Larson, MD, illustrates how some people are affected by amputation:

"The surgical removal of a body part also can be an emotionally demanding event. There may be pain in the stump or the sensation, sometimes painful, that the limb or part of the limb is still present, so called phantom limb pain. In addition, your self image, *self confidence* and self worth may be affected. . . . In addition to drawing on the body's healing capacity, an amputation also requires a *significant psychological adjustment*." [Emphasis added.]

There is no doubt that confidence is diminished in the declawed cat, and many cat owners report that their cat's personality changed drastically after being declawed. Many owners of declawed cats are disappointed, and most tell me they would never have it done again.

true story

I knew a woman who spent $800 to have her cat's feet fixed after the cat had been declawed. Loose bones caused some claws to become infected. A couple of claws even tried to grow back, and required more surgery. This veterinarian bill cost even more than the price of her sofa and bed, both of which had been damaged by cat urine.

Still Considering Declawing?

If you really think declawing will save you time and money, ask your veterinarian for answers to these questions before you sign up for the operation:

- Will she guarantee that your declawed cat won't start peeing? Will she pay for the urine tests, neutralizers, or damage? Will she guarantee that your cat's personality won't change? Or that he won't become a biter?
- Is there risk of infection, a second operation, or diabetes? How much will that cost? (Sometimes pieces of loose bone can cause infection, requiring subsequent operations.)
- How will you exercise a declawed cat? How much time was spent in veterinarian school discussing ways to exercise cats? Were considerations taken into account for the cat being handicapped?
- How many declawed cats has she euthanized for a litter box problem?
- If your cat is being declawed because the veterinarian claims it will make the cat less "dangerous," ask how dangerous it could be if he pees all over the place. Declawing will not make a cat

less dangerous. Besides, if the cat is so "dangerous" that surgery is necessary, remember that there are millions of cats being euthanized every year due to lack of homes that are not dangerous and won't require expensive surgery.

Did You Know?
▶ Declawing is the removal of bones, tendons, ligaments, and claws to the first knuckle of each toe.

▶ Declawing undermines the health, and consequently the behavior, of the cat.

▶ Declawing can lead to worse problems.

▶ Declawing has only started in about the last forty years. Clawed cats have been living indoors much longer than that.

Declawing Isn't the Only Bad Idea

A tendonectomy is a relatively new surgical procedure that severs the tendon in each toe. The cat will not be able to control or extend his claws. You still will have to trim his claws. He'll be unable to perform his much-needed scratching, pulling, and tugging exercise. He could face years with painful feet and bear the same litter box or biting problems as his amputee brothers. *Do not choose this option.* Even though no amputation takes place, torn or cut tendons are very painful. In people, a torn tendon in the foot can take years to heal.

Afraid of Getting Scratched? ■ Avoid adopting a declawed cat. If you are so afraid of claws, cats—as well as dogs, birds, and many other pets—are not for you.

Moses's Story

While writing this book, I had to have one of my own cats put to sleep. Moses was a beautiful black-and-white, declawed cat.

He was picked up as a stray and taken to a shelter. On the fifth day he was scheduled for euthanasia. Minutes before being destroyed he was rescued by a local shelter volunteer. I took him in as a foster cat. He had wrinkled pads on his mutilated feet.

He wasn't suitable for adoption. He peed in the bathroom sink and a couple of other spots that were not a litter box. He would bite my hands at the slightest movement. He was easily stressed and quick to hiss. He whined when he scratched. He pawed at the area around his box longer than his buddies did.

Groups Opposed to Declawing

▶ The Paw Project (1-877-PAWPROJECT; *www.pawproject.com*)
▶ The British Veterinary Association
▶ The Royal College of Veterinary Surgeons
▶ Cats International (*www.catsinternational.org*)
▶ In Defense of Animals (*www.idausa.org*). IDA opposes declawing, and in its publications states, "The excuses people use for wanting to declaw a cat are usually trivial, and nearly always put the well-being of their belongings above that of the cat."
▶ Friends of Animals (*www.friendsofanimals.org*): "If you love your cat, don't declaw."
▶ Animal Protection Institute (*www.api4animals.org*): "Please make the humane choice—do not declaw."

See *www.pawproject.com* for more organizations that oppose declawing.

Many things were different about him. And I knew he had been abused because he paid such close attention to hands and squirt bottles. It took several months to get his biting under control. In an attempt to solve his peeing problem, I took him to a few different doctors for urine tests and examinations. I talked with a behaviorist.

After many suggestions, Moses was still misbehaving. I started thinking about how amputee humans deal with their pain and stress, and I applied similar techniques to him. My special regime, which is detailed in Chapter 21, kept his peeing problem at bay for about two years.

Then his peeing became more frequent and less isolated to certain spots. He peed in my dresser, on my desk, in the bed, even on my husband's neck once while he slept. Some days were worse than others. Moses appeared to want attention, but a closer look told me he was in pain. It kept getting worse. I took him to another veterinarian. Then Moses started peeing on carpet. That's when I knew it was time to have him put out of his misery. Moses was peacefully put to sleep. He was only three-and-a-half years old.

If Moses had his claws, he could have lived outside. I do not believe declawed cats should be kept outside or left there unsupervised. I also don't believe it's healthy or safe to live with cat urine problems inside the house. And I did not want to return a peeing cat to a shelter, all of which are burdened enough with *good* cats. Besides, he might get a home with people who would abandon him (which may be how he lost his first home). I believe he was suffering. I loved him way too much for the options left to him.

Did You Know?

▶ Litter box problems are the reason for nearly all of the calls I get from declawed-cat owners. Clawed-cat owners call me for a wide variety of reasons.

▶ Most owners of declawed cats report litter box problems beginning at earlier ages, usually before the cat is eight.

▶ Clawed-cat litter box problems typically begin later in life and usually are caused by a medical condition.

I had named him Moses because declawing makes a cat a slave to his disability and makes the cat owner a slave to the disabled cat. In the end, it's the owner who becomes slave to the litter box, to the biting, to illness—burdened with chores and bills that should never have been.

I wanted Moses here with me when this book came out to show you just how smart he was. I taught him tricks in just a few lessons.

He came running when I called for him. Moses wasn't an attack cat. Declawing didn't save his life, and it probably caused his litter box problems. It limited his and my options and paved the way both for his initial abandonment and then for his death.

My tribute to Moses was to find another cat that needed a home. The day after Moses died, and with eyes swollen from crying, I went to a shelter in Denver and found a big, black-and-white three-year-old. He gets along just fine with my other three adult cats. He has beautiful, whole feet and is smart, as most cats are.

I named my new cat Abraham Lincoln in hopes that American cats will be free someday: free from the burden of being permanently disabled. Cats never used to need antidepressants or fancy litters. Cats didn't used to pee outside the box until they got sick or old. Then declawing came along.

Declawing Resources
For more information on declawing I recommend the following sources.

Books
The Shocking Truth About Declawing Cats (That Most Veterinarians Don't Acknowledge or Tell) by Harriet Baker (The Cat Catalyst, Inc., 2000.)

Send $23 (includes $3 S&H) to:
The Cat Catalyst, Inc.
613 Sea Street
Quincy, MA 02169-2811
Phone: (617) 472-9618

Organizations

The Paw Project is a nonprofit organization dedicated to ending declawing.

The Paw Project
P.O. Box 445
Santa Monica, CA 90406-0445
www.pawproject.com
Phone: 1-877-PAWPROJECT (1-877-729-7765)
Outside USA, 1 (310) 795-6215

Web Sites

www.declawing.com

www.stopdeclaw.com

www.declaw.com (lists veterinarians who don't declaw)

www.listnow.com/helpingpaws/

http://declaw.lisaviolet.com

http://maxshouse.com/Truth%20About%20Declawing.htm

www.declawhallofshame.com

http://avar.org/avar_summer_2001_directions.pdf. See pages 2–3 for an article about declawed cats.

Expert Opinions
What others say about declawing:

"Climbing is another part of the cat's normal behavior repertoire. Some cats climb up the curtains, e.g., to reach an elevated resting place, to escape, or in the course of hunting insects and playing. The operative removal of the claws, as is sometimes practiced to protect furniture and curtains, is an act of abuse and should be forbidden by law in all, not just a few countries."
                    —authors Dennis C. Turner and Patrick Bateson
                        in *The Domestic Cat: The Biology of Its Behavior*

"I, for one, would like to see declawing or "claw modification" banned as an inhumane and unnecessary mutilation. . . . words such as deform, disfigure, disjoint and dismember all apply to this surgery. Partial digital amputation is so horrible that it has been employed for torture of prisoners of war."
                    —Dr. Nicholas Dodman, BVMS, MRCVSm DACVB,
                        Professor, Section Head and Program Director,
                        Animal Behavior, Department of Clinical Sciences,
                        Tufts University School of Veterinary Medicine,
                        author of *The Cat Who Cried for Help*

Did You Know? ▧ Declawing is illegal or considered inhumane in Australia, Austria, Belgium, Brazil, Denmark, Finland, France, Germany, Ireland, Italy, Japan, Netherlands, New Zealand, North Ireland, Norway, Portugal, Scotland, Slovenia, Sweden, Switzerland, the United Kingdom (Britain), Wales, and Yugoslavia—and the list keeps growing. (See *www.declawing.com*.)

"The request itself {declawing} is an indication that the household is not suitable for a cat."
                    —Dr. Louis J. Camuti, DVM

"I'm tired of all the calls I get telling me that they need to get rid of their cat because all of a sudden it won't use the litter box or it is biting. My first question is always, "When did you declaw your cat?"

—Rene Knapp, president of Helping Paws,
a local rescue organization based in Colchester, Connecticut
(visit *www.listnow.com/helpingpaws/*)

"The Royal College of Veterinary Surgeons (RCVS) regards the procedure as an unethical mutilation."

—C J Laurence, QVRM TD BVSc MRCVS,
Chief Veterinary Officer of the Royal Society
for the Prevention of Cruelty to Animals

"Declawing is a truly barbaric, disabling mutilation and should not even be thought of as a means of control for this problem. . . . This barbaric, unnecessary operation has become common in the United States. This mutilation of millions of cats is a real cost that needs considering when policy statements are made by welfare groups about captive cats. Fortunately, the British Veterinary Association and the Royal College of Veterinary Surgeons are firmly against declawing, and consequently it is not allowed in Britain."

—author Roger Tabor in
Understanding Cats: Their History, Nature, and Behavior

"Some say it's minor surgery. Others say X rays of the bone structure of Kitty's legs before and after declawing show a marked difference that's caused by his having to balance himself unnaturally. Without the nails, physical stress is placed on the legs, where it wasn't intended to be."

—authors Warren Eckstein and Fay Eckstein in
How to Get Your Cat to Do What You Want

"Declawing is a cruel practice, deplored by animal welfare organizations and caring veterinarians."

—author Chris Madsen in *Natural Cats*

"A recently published translation of a German book says that declawing is punishable under German animal protective law, and concludes, 'A cat without its natural weapons is like every other creature enslaved by man—it is no longer itself!'"

—author Roz Riddle in
The City Cat: How to Live Healthily and Happily with Your Indoor Pet

Did You Know? ■ If a veterinarian says he has a study that says declawing has no side effects, scrutinize the validity of the data: Over what time frame was the study conducted? Was data collected five, ten, twenty years later? What age groups were studied? Were injuries, illness, diseases, and behavior problems such as litter box problems recorded?

"Many veterinarians refuse to mutilate cats in this way. Undoubtedly, these veterinarians have learned through experience what can happen if their four-footed patients slip outside after being declawed. No longer able to escape or defend themselves, the cats are brought back to the veterinarians to be sewn up or euthanized after being attacked by other animals."

author Terry Jester in *Train Your Cat*

"A declawed cat's emotional reaction to the surgery can trigger various chronic physical ailments, such as cystitis, skin disorders, and asthma."

—author Carole C. Wilbourn in
*Cats on the Couch:
The Complete Guide for Loving and Caring for Your Cat*

"The physical effect of declawing is gradual weakening of the muscles of the legs, shoulders, and back. Balance is impaired. The cat is 75 percent defenseless."

—author Anitra Frazier with Norma Eckroate in
The New Natural Cat: A Complete Guide for Finicky Owners

"The practice of [declawing] is not only cruel and painful, but it also prevents the important feline exercise pattern of kneading and stretching, which benefits the muscles of the forelegs, backbone and shoulders. A cat that can't perform this ritual can become weaker and thus more susceptible to illness and degeneration. It can impair a cat's balance, weaken it (from muscular disuse) and cause it to feel nervous and defenseless. The resulting stress can lower its immunity to disease and make it more likely to be a biter."

—authors Richard H. Pitcairn, DVM, PhD,
and Susan Hubble Pitcairn in
Dr. Pitcairn's Complete Guide to Natural Health for Dogs & Cats

Cute Cat Tricks

🐾 I have mixed emotions about tricks—I don't really approve
of them for cats. One reason is because professionally trained
tricksters must be kept hungry to perform. Also, I think that teaching an animal to do tricks compromises its dignity, especially if the
animal is a cat.

But everyone loved it when my Moses did tricks. He learned
them in a day or two and became a polished performer after about a
month of one-minute lessons. It occurred to me that if I could teach
Moses to do these, how difficult could it be to get a cat to use the
scratching post? If you teach these tricks, try to end each training
session on a well-performed command. Don't wait until your cat is
bored or tired. And don't expect him to perform the same trick more
than ten times in a row. For that reason, you should keep each training session under sixty seconds, repeated one to three times a day.

The "What It Is" Trick

Also known as the "give me five" or "shake hands" trick.

1. Find a place to train your cat that is up off the floor, such as a
   tabletop. Having the cat higher up is easier on the trainer and
   puts the cat into "training mode" as well.

2. Wait until your cat is hungry, such as before his regularly scheduled wet meal.

3. Have a few special food treats that he likes, but doesn't normally get, at hand.

4. Call your cat to come for his meal, and give him a small treat when he arrives.

5. Put the second treat in your right hand.

6. Using his name, say "What it is?" Hold your right hand out but slightly away from him so that he has to use his paw to reach the food. When his paw touches or gets close to your right hand, give him the treat.

7. Repeat until your cat begins to touch your hand regularly. After the third day, don't give him a treat if he only comes close.

8. Once he begins touching your right hand, put the treat in your left hand but still have your cat touch your right hand. Don't give him any treat unless he touches your right hand.

9. Start requiring him to always use the same paw (left or right) to "shake hands" with.

10. Occasionally, make your cat perform this command, and other commands, without food and just before he is allowed outside.

true story

In his younger days, Bob used to fetch paper balls without getting any food treats. He enjoyed getting praised and petted as his reward.

The "Gimme Some" Command

Also known as the "kiss me" trick. Moses would reach his little face up to mine and it was so cute!

1. Only do this with a cat that won't claw or bite your cheek in order to get to some food. Follow the same procedure as above, but wait for him to sniff or touch your face (instead of touching

your hand as taught in the previous trick) before giving him the treat. Try using a bit of baby food smeared on your cheek. The closer he gets to your cheek, the sooner he should get his treat.

2. Once he's been successful, don't settle for less. Always require him to touch your face in a certain place to get his treat.

3. As time goes on, make him reach farther to kiss you.

Helpful Hints ▪ Not every cat will perform tricks, but if you have a cat that likes food, outdoor time, or playing, then he'll probably be able to learn one trick or another. Going outside, playing with you or receiving special food treats are great motivators for cats to learn tricks. For example, my cats *love* being outdoors, when they want to go out I have them scratch the post first.

A cat that has a tendency to use her paws, mouth, or voice is likely to learn tricks that use those parts. Make up your own tricks. But avoid teaching a cat to "sit." It's boring and beneath them.

Cat Maintenance Schedule

Adoption
- ❏ spay/neuter—*do not* declaw
- ❏ leukemia test
- ❏ examination by veterinarian
- ❏ distemper shot
- ❏ rabies shot (ask your veterinarian about rabies shots that are less likely to cause cancer)
- ❏ trim claws
- ❏ give vitamins
- ❏ microchip and tattoo cat (*www.tattoo-a-pet.com*)
- ❏ post sign in window for firemen; specify how many cats are inside
- ❏ make provisions in will for cats (*www.3arkangels.com*)

Daily
- ❏ talk to/say name/praise
- ❏ encourage use of scratching post
- ❏ feed wet food
- ❏ provide fresh water
- ❏ play and/or walk outside
- ❏ touch/pet

- ❏ brush daily if needed
- ❏ lift solids and shake litter box—more frequently for a declawed cat
- ❏ massage cat; especially declawed, very young, sick, elderly, or foster cats

Weekly
- ❏ dump and fill box with new litter (or as directed by cat litter manufacturer)—more frequently for old or sick cats, declawed cats, or multiple-cat households
- ❏ wash box—more often for a declawed cat
- ❏ check condition of litter box area and condition of cat beds
- ❏ feed organic catnip—once a week; twice or more weekly for a declawed cat
- ❏ brush weekly during shedding season or if the cat is elderly
- ❏ administer hairball remedy

Monthly
- ❏ trim nails
- ❏ brush
- ❏ buy cat food and litter
- ❏ wash water bowl with soapy water; rinse well
- ❏ wash/clean cat beds
- ❏ rotate cat toys (hide toys that your cat is currently bored with; retrieve old cat toys from storage)

Yearly
- ❏ examination by veterinarian
- ❏ inspect feet of declawed cat
- ❏ inspect and clean ears—more often for double-declawed cat

❑ inspect teeth for brown tartar
❑ note sleeping, eating, drinking, and litter box habits
❑ new cat toys
❑ new cat bed
❑ inspect scratching posts for usage, replacement
❑ update will/instructions to friends/lawyer (what to do with your cat)
❑ take a vacation away from your cat

As Needed (these things usually last for years)
❑ vaccinations (see note below)
❑ re-cover old tree or buy new cat tree and scratching post
❑ cat door replacement (swinging door for outside access)
❑ litter box replacement

Note: My Personal Belief About Vaccines

Many holistic veterinarians feel that pets are being overvaccinated. I agree. Without definitive research, however, these are only personal beliefs. Decide what you want for your cat. Keeping in mind your local laws and community responsibilities, do what you think is best.

● Ask your veterinarian about vaccines that are suspected of causing cancer or other serious side effects.
● Keep rabies vaccinations current.
● After the initial distemper shots, only revaccinate at age ten.
● Avoid feline leukemia shots. The vaccine offers no guarantees, so why spend the money?
● If at all possible, don't vaccinate a cat that's over the age of twelve.
● Don't vaccinate a sick or nursing cat.
● A cat should be healthy and fully recovered from surgery before getting vaccinated.

Cat Advocacy

 If you'd like to help cats in general, there are many things you can do.

Animal Shelters

Hundreds of animal shelters across the country could use volunteer help as well as donations. Ask about the volunteer positions they have, or specific areas that interest you. Many shelters have a wide variety of volunteer needs; these are just a few of the things that you might do:

- Foster cats in your home.
- Write newsletters, stuff envelopes, make phone calls.
- Walk and handle caged cats; clean kennels.
- Manage the front desk.
- Take cats or dogs to visit patients in nursing homes.

If you don't have the time to volunteer, cat shelters appreciate donations of cat food, money, books, litter boxes, rubbing alcohol, heating pads, towels, and all sorts of other stuff. Some shelters also have thrift stores or rummage sales to raise money, and welcome your sellable castoffs.

Help Keep Cats Out of Laboratories

In the book *Why Animal Experiments Must Stop*, Vernon Coleman estimates that worldwide, 100,000 to 125,000 animals are used in experiments every hour. In the United States, according to Coleman, an animal dies every three seconds in laboratories. Many will be cats. In reality, this figure may be conservative, because some laboratories are secretive about their efforts. The conditions are unbearable, with cats confined to cages so small they can't stand or stretch. Many experiments are conducted without painkillers or anesthesia. You can help discourage such practices in these ways:

- Buy products that aren't tested on animals. There are many companies that won't use animals to test their cosmetics or household cleaners.
- Write to your senator or state representative concerning lab-animal issues. *www.votesmart.org*
- Get your cat tattooed and urge others to do so. It's a federal offense for a laboratory to accept or test on tattooed animals. (See the Products and Resources section of this Appendix for more about tattooing.)

For more information about what you can do to save animals from inhumane testing procedures, contact:

The American Anti-Vivisection Society (AAVS)
801 Old York Road #204
Jenkintown, PA 19046-1685 USA
Phone: 215-887-0816
www.aavs.org

Society for Animal Protection Legislation (SAPL)
Division of Animal Welfare Institute (AWI)
P.O. Box 3650
Washington, DC 20027
Phone: 703-836-4300
Fax: 703-836-0400
www.awionline.org
www.saplonline.org

Help Stop Declawing

Declawing is a disabling procedure performed on cats by veterinarians, mostly in the United States. It is illegal or considered inhumane in several countries.

- Ask your veterinarian to stop declawing.
- Patronize veterinarians who refuse to declaw.
- Support The Paw Project, a nonprofit organization dedicated to ending declawing.

Contact:

The Paw Project
Phone: 1-877-PAWPROJECT (1-877-729-7765)
Outside USA, 1 (310) 795-6215
www.pawproject.com

● Ask the American Veterinary Medical Association (AVMA) to record/count/track/recognize the cats that are already declawed in *all* cat research.

Contact:

American Veterinary Medical Association (AVMA)
Attn: Animal Welfare Committee
AVMA Schaumburg Office
1931 N. Meacham Rd., Suite 100
Schaumburg, IL 60173-4360
Phone: (800) 248-2862
Fax: 847-925-1329
www.avma.org

● Have AVAR send information to veterinarians who declaw. *www.avar.org/catdeclawbrochure.pdf*

The Association of Veterinarians for Animal Rights (AVAR)
P.O. Box 208
Davis, CA 95617-0208
Phone: 530-759-8106
Fax: 530-759-8116
www.avar.org

● **Adopt clawed cats only.** Adopting a clawed cat is the *easiest* way you can help end declawing. Declawed cats are like cigarettes—they're dangerous and you can't buy one without supporting *the* industry that profits from making them. Don't give veterinarians *any* reason to manufacture more declawed cats. There are *millions* of smart, trainable clawed cats that need homes. Save your time, energy, and home for clawed cats only.

Help Other Cat Owners

The more you learn about cat behavior, the more you can help others improve the relationship they have with their cats.

- Talk with other cat owners. You can get into cat discussion groups on the Internet.
- Wear cat-themed clothes around town. When people ask about your cats, you can tell them what you know.
- Copy this chapter, "How to Have a Good Cat" and "Important Facts About Declawed Cats" pages at the end of this book and give them to others.

Help Feral Cats

"Feral" means "wild." Feral cats either grew up wild or turned wild after being lost or abandoned. They live in feral "colonies" with other wild cats. Sometimes a person or a group will act as a "caretaker" for a colony. Caretakers provide food and water and occasionally a small shelter, as well as spaying or neutering of the entire colony. Cared-for ferals can live as long as ten years; without a caretaker, they will live only about two years. As long as they aren't breeding and are left alone, they pose no threat to humans.

A feral cat is hardly ever suitable for adoption as a pet. Some owners have had success retraining feral cats, but it took years. Some semi-ferals are able to adjust if caught soon enough. It's best to let ferals live with their own kind. Ferals do not need your home. Ferals *are* at home in the wild.

Why Be Concerned About Feral Cats?

If feral cats continue to breed and multiply, their numbers "swell quickly to unmanageable magnitude," according to Esther Mechler, director of SPAY/USA in New York. That's no lie: One female cat and her offspring theoretically can produce 420,000 cats in seven years. This problem becomes everyone's responsibility. Without the tireless efforts of volunteers and veterinarians who trap and alter cats, our cities would be overrun with cats.

Destroying feral cats only keeps a steady stream of new cats invading the area. However, if an entire colony is trapped, altered, and returned to the same area, their numbers remain steady. Some cities and counties pledge funds to control the population—a form of "animal control." The results have paid off. Studies across the United States and Europe have shown not only that the stray cat population is decreasing, but that it is actually cheaper to spay, neuter, and return ferals to their colony than it is to kill them.

About Feral Cats

▶ Never touch or handle a feral cat.

▶ Feral cats usually make bad house pets. Ferals live in and prefer the outdoors. They do not consider your home a paradise—to them, it's a prison.

▶ There are about 60 million feral cats in the United States alone. About 17.5 million Americans feed feral cats.

▶ If a feral is returned to a different colony, he may try to return "home" even if it takes crossing several miles of highways to do it.

What to Do If You Find a Feral Cat Colony

A few shelters may know the location of feral colonies and caretakers in your area. Because some agencies simply kill feral cats and others offer assistance, call different shelters. Ask about organizations whose mission is to spay and neuter feral cats. Some shelters will trap, alter, and return the colony *if* the caller or community can locate a caretaker who will commit to feeding and watering the colony every day. Backup caretakers also are needed. Shelters don't like to return fixed ferals to an area that has no steady food and water supply because the cats won't live long under those conditions. SPAY/USA and Alley Cat Allies have a growing friends-of-feral-felines national network. They can help you organize your community.

Setting Up Your Own Spay/Neutering of Ferals

If you cannot locate a shelter that will fund the operation, collect donations in the neighborhood and then pay a low-cost clinic to do the procedures. Your local shelter might provide the traps if you leave a refundable deposit. This takes serious dedication and commitment, but it can be done.

A booklet called *Feral Friends: A Guide for Living with Feral Cats*, by Audrey Boag, describes how to trap and tame ferals, and also includes a lot of other information. You can order the booklet by sending $6.00 to:

Audrey Boag
P.O. Box 714
Conifer, CO 80433

What Else You Can Do for Ferals

Raise community awareness. Ferals are easy targets on which to vent abuse.

● Set a good example for kids. Let them know that anyone who tortures cats or other animals is doing something very wrong and needs a mental health professional.
● Volunteer to feed and water a cat colony. You must be able to go to the colony every day and have a backup for any day you cannot make it.
● Volunteer to trap ferals and transport them to the vet's office to be altered. Then transport them back to the colony.
● If you see a cat roaming the neighborhood that doesn't appear to be taken care of, consider calling the shelter to have him rescued. Some people will agree to have a stray altered and then find him another home. Neighborhood cats are no longer anyone's pet. They don't have regular proper care, but they are *not yet* feral. When caught and fixed soon enough in life, a

neighborhood stray is quite adoptable. But if he runs the streets with little or no human contact, he will lose trust and become feral in no time.

Contact List for Spay and Neutering Services

For information on veterinarians closest to you offering affordable spay and neutering services, contact:

SPAY/USA
P.O. Box 801
Trumbull, CT 06611
Phone: 1-800 248-SPAY (7729)
www.spayusa.org

Alley Cat Allies
1801 Belmont Road N.W., Suite 201
Washington, DC 20009
Phone: 202-667-3630
www.alleycat.org

Donations Needed

 I like too many organizations to list, but these are some of my favorites. All of them gratefully accept donations.

SPAY/USA

The mission of SPAY/USA is to end pet overpopulation. SPAY/USA is a network of volunteers and veterinarians working together to popularize and facilitate spay/neuter services through a nationwide toll-free referral service. SPAY/USA empowers local groups to start their own spay/neuter clinics.

> SPAY/USA
> P.O. Box 801
> Trumbull, CT 06611
> Phone: 1-800 248-SPAY (7729)
> *www.spayusa.org*

The Paw Project

The Paw Project is a nonprofit organization dedicated to ending declawing. The Paw Project exists to increase public awareness of animal welfare issues related to the crippling effects of feline declawing, to rehabilitate big cats that have been declawed, and to abolish the practice of declaw surgery.

The Paw Project
P.O. Box 445
Santa Monica, CA 90406-0445
Phone 1-877-PAWPROJECT (1-877-729-7765)
Outside USA, 1 (310) 795-6215
www.pawproject.com

Helping Paws

Helping Paws is a nonprofit, charitable organization dedicated to saving the lives of abandoned, abused, and neglected animals, getting them medical care, and placing them into good adoptive homes.

Helping Paws, Inc.
P.O. Box 476
Colchester, CT 06415-0476
Phone: 860-267-0496
www.listnow.com/helpingpaws/

Alley Cat Allies

Alley Cat Allies operates a network that links individuals together and helps educate the public about the humane techniques available for managing feral cat colonies.

Alley Cat Allies
1801 Belmont Road N.W., Suite 201
Washington, DC 20009
Phone: 202-667-3630
www.alleycat.org

Cats International

Cats International is a nonprofit educational organization dedicated to helping people better understand their feline companions. It offers advice for feline behavior problems and answers questions absolutely free!

> **Cats International**
> 193 Granville Road
> Cedarburg, WI 53012
> Behavior hotline: 262-375-8852
> *www.catsinternational.org*

Good Samaritan Pet Center

Good Samaritan Pet Center is a nonprofit animal rescue organization that provides a "shelter alternative" for homeless animals throughout the Denver metro area. Good Samaritan has a network of foster parents who care for these animals until a permanent home can be found. The organization's mission is to promote healthy relationships between people and their pets. Good Samaritan strives to prevent animal abuse and abandonment and to provide resources and support services to fulfill its goals.

> **Good Samaritan Pet Center**
> P.O. Box 202005
> Denver, CO 80220
> Phone: 303-333-2291
> Fax: 303-377-1625
> *www.GoodSamaritanPetCenter.org*

Products and Resources

I buy a lot of cat stuff and get help from a lot of resources. There's no room to list all of them; these are some of my favorites. Most companies will send you a free catalog or information. (Information about cat foods, cat litters, and urine neutralizers appears separately within this section of the Appendix.)

Recommended Resources

Things I Buy	Where I Buy Them
Felix Katnip Trees These are covered with sisal fabric and are favorites for my cats. My cats have scratched on Felix posts for years and the posts still look new!	The Felix Company 3623 Fremont Ave. N, Seattle, WA 98103 206-547-0042 *www.felixkatniptreecompany.com*
Tattoos and registry number (see the Tattooing notes on the next page)	TATOO-A-PET 6571 SW. 20th Court Ft. Lauderdale, FL 33317 1-800-TATTOOS (828-8667) *www.tattoo-a-pet.com*

Things I Buy	Where I Buy Them
Convincing pet driver's license with your cat's picture and statistics; comes in different U.S. state licenses. These makes great gifts. Cat owners get a kick out 'em!	Chloe Cards 1118 13th St. Dept 25-B Boulder, CO 80302 In Colorado 303-442-7790 1-888-245-6388 (toll free) *www.chloecards.com*
Great gifts for cat lovers—books, clothes, home décor, videos, and more	*www.cattycorner.com*
Pet supplies: cat trees, toys, combs, brushes, carrier cases, collars, catnip, hairball remedies, black light, litter mats, videos for cats to watch, etc.	pet stores; mail order; animal shelters; grocery stores; hardware stores Double 'S' Enterprises serving feline fanciers 1-888-779-DBLS *www.double-s.com* Drs. Foster & Smith comprehensive catalog for cat supplies 1-800-826-7206 *www.drsfostersmith.com*
Neutralizer for cat urine (see special section below)	hardware stores; pet stores Mother Nature's Odor Remover, *www.mothernaturesodor.com* Get Serious! Stain, odor, and pheromone extractor, *www.getseriousproducts.com*. X-O Odor Neutralizer, natural and organic, *www.xocorp.com*. Especially for Cats Stain & Odor Remover, manufactured by Venus Pet Products, 1-800-592-1900 Urine-Off, Odor & Stain Remover, *www.urine-off.com*

Things I Buy	Where I Buy Them
Cat litter and litter accessories (see special section in this Appendix and in Chapter 7)	grocery stores, pet stores: PETCO PETsMART
Organic catnip, scratching pads, cat supplies, kitty oats, toys	Cats Claws 1-800-783-0977 www.CatClaws.com
Cat harness	The SureFit Harness works great! Does not tug on neck, makes for comfortable cat walks. www.premier.com
Cat food (see Cat Food Contact List in this Appendix)	Natural pet food stores Health food stores such as Whole Foods and Wild Oats
Vitamins for cats (Tasha's Herbs for cats come in wide variety of formulas)	health food stores Tasha's Herbs Coyote Springs Naturals, Inc. 1150 Deer Run Road Prescott, AZ 86303 1-800-315-0142
Bach Flower Rescue Remedy	health food stores
SpiritEssence-Energy Remedies for Animals and Their People — flower essence remedies	720-938-6794; www.spiritessence.com
European-Style Pet Food Mix for Cats (a grains mix you add to homemade or canned food or plain yogurt)	Sojourner Farms 1-888-TO-SOJOS (867-6567) (toll free) www.sojos.com

Things I Buy	Where I Buy Them
Natural pet food supplements	Urban King www.UrbanWolf.cc Ark Naturals 1-800-926-5100 www.arknaturals.com Nature's Menu 1-866-FEED-RAW (333-3729) www.naturesmenu.com Wysong, www.wysong.net Anitra's Vita-Mineral Mix, www.halopets.com
Hairball remedies	Cat-Lube Hairball & Digestive Aid by Veterinarian's Best, 1-800-866-PETS, www.vetsbest.com Hair Ball Gel by Vetbasis, 1-888-414-7387, www.vetbasis.com
Green Herb—great natural herbs for humans and pets.	Green Herb, LLC 8041 I-70 Frontage Road, #11 Arvada, CO 80002 Denver Metro Area 303-421-9900 1-888-765-HERB (765-4372) (toll free) www.thegreenherb.com
Heavy fabric or plastic to protect sofa; crochet hook to repair snags; twist upholstery pins to attach protection to sofa	fabric store, hardware store
Cardboard scratching pad (great price!)	Trader Joes, 1-800-SHOP-TJS 1-800-746-7857 www.traderjoes.com

Things I Buy	Where I Buy Them
Sticky Paws For Furniture wide double-stick tape to deter cats from scratching the sofa	Fe-Lines, Inc. 2924 6th Ave., Fort Worth TX 76110 1-888-697-2873 *www.stickypaws.com*
Motion sensitive pet deterrents	Contech Electronics Inc. 6582 Bryn Road Victoria, BC V8M 1X6 Canada Toll free 1-800-767-8658 *www.scatmat.com*
Carpet cleaner for cat vomit	vacuum stores; carpet cleaning companies
Digital thermometer; a roll of nonskid rubber mat, useful for keeping things on shelves that cats normally knock off; underpads	drug stores or discount stores Target
Preparing your pets for the future Helping you and your pets prepare for the unexpected.	*www.3arkangels.com*

Tattooing

More than 2 million dogs and cats are stolen each year and sold to labs. Half of tattooed cats and nearly all tattooed dogs are recovered when lost. The tattoo takes just minutes and lasts forever.

How to Get It Done

1. Tatoo-A-Pet is a well-known pet tattoo registry. Call Tatoo-A-Pet at 1-800-TATTOOS (828-8667) and ask for the phone number of the tattoo agent closest to you. *www.tattoo-a-pet.com*

2. Make an appointment with the tattoo agent.
3. Get a tranquilizer pill from the vet. Ask when you should administer it to your cat. You may not need to sedate your cat, but it's good to be prepared.
4. Take a large beach towel and pillow case to restrain the cat while he's being tattooed. You probably will need to assist the tattoo agent during the procedure; two people usually are needed to steady a cat that is not heavily sedated.
5. Have a cat tattooed in his ear unless he's a show cat. To be extra cautious you can also tattoo him on his inner thigh; some cats have shown up for sale to laboratories with an ear cut off. (Dogs usually are tattooed on the inner thigh, where there is little hair.) The tattoo agent will use a registration code that will be traced back to you should your animal be picked up as a lost pet.
6. The tattoo agent will register your cat's code with Tatoo-A-Pet. You can now use 1-800-TATTOOS as the phone number on your cat collar instead of your home phone number if you want to. Tatoo-A-Pet also will provide identification tags for a small fee.

What Not to Buy When Owning Cats

Avoid furniture with rough surfaces, such as tapestry or wicker. Roughness will tempt cats to scratch. Velours are slippery and not so easy to snag. If you are not sure how the fabric of a new sofa will stand up to snags, get a sample of it, take it home, and try to destroy it. If you can snag it by stroking it with a wire brush or steel nails, it's probably not a wise purchase.

Cats also can easily destroy terry-cloth bath robes, foam rubber, dried flower arrangements, grassy house plants, sheer drapes, and feathered ornament plants.

Cat Food Contact List

Breeder's Choice Pet Foods, makers of Pinnacle, Avo-Derm Cat Food, and Advance Pet Diets (APD). 1-800-255-4AVO (255-4286), *www.breeders-choice.com*

Felidae, All Natural Cat & Kitten Formula. 1-800-398-1600, *www.canidae.com*

Flint River Ranch Cat and Kitten food. Holistic veterinarians might carry this food. 1243 Columbia Ave., B-6, Riverside, CA 92507. 1-800-704-5779, *www.flintriver-home.com*

Merrick Petfoods, Inc., 1-800-664-PETS (7387), Fax 806-364-6530, *www.merrickpetcare.com*

Natures Variety, makers of Prairie canned, dry, freeze dried, and raw pet foods, *www.naturesvariety.com*

One Earth, 1-800-8-EARTHY (832-7849)

Organix Feline Formula, 1-800-875-7518, *www.castorpolluxpet.com*

PetGuard, makers of canned and dry pet food, 1-800-874-3221, *www.petguard.com*

Precise, makers of canned and dry food, 1-800-446-7148, *www.precisepet.com*

Spots Stew, manufactured for Halo Purely for Pets, 3433 East Lake Rd., Suite 14, Palm Harbor, FL 34685. Halo Purely for Pets carries catnip, food supplements, and other natural pet products. 1-800-426-4256, *www.halopets.com*

Wysong has information, food supplements, and different varieties of canned, dry, and freeze-dried pet foods, including a formula for urinary tract problems. Wysong Corporation, 1880 N. Eastman, Midland, MI 48642. 1-800-748-0188, *www.wysong.net*

Cat Litters Contact List

These litters were mentioned in chapters concerning litter and are found in many pet stores.

World's Best Cat Litter—natural clumping litter

1-877-367-9225
www.worldsbestcatlitter.com

SWHEAT SCOOP Wheat Litter

Pet Care Systems, Inc.
1-800-SWHEATS
www.swheatscoop.com

Here's the Scoop! Clumping Cat Litter

Integrated Pet Foods, Inc.
1-800-542-4677
www.integratedpet.com

CatWorks, The Premium Cat Litter

Absorption Corp.
1051 Hilton Ave.
Bellingham, WA 98225
www.absorbent.com

Feline Pine—100 percent kiln-dried southern yellow pine

Nature's Earth Products, Inc.
1-800-749-PINE
www.naturesearth.com

Neutralizer Product List

These neutralizers are found at most pet stores, some hardware stores, and by mail order. Read the labels for instructions.

● Especially for Cats Stain & Odor Remover, manufactured by Venus Pet Products, 1-800-592-1900

- Get Serious! Stain, odor, and pheromone extractor, 714-639-3580, *www.getseriousproducts.com*
- Mother Nature's Odor Remover, 1-800-333-7254, *www.mother naturesodor.com*
- Urine-Off, Odor & Stain Remover, *www.urine-off.com*
- X-O Odor Neutralizer, natural and organic, *www.xocorp.com*

Cat Behavior Consulting

To find cat behavior help, call your local animal shelter or pet store; they often know consultants in the area. Ask your veterinarian or pet sitter. Try the yellow pages under "Cat Products, Services." Look for behaviorists who don't recommend declawing. The behaviorists listed below are happy to take your calls and e-mails and answer your questions:

Mr. Jackson Galaxy, Feline Behavior Consultant

Little Big Cat, Inc.—Mind/Body Consultations for Cats and Their People

Jackson is a great guy who knows and cares about cats. I recommend him highly.

Mr. Jackson Galaxy
P.O. Box 18976
Boulder, CO 80308
Phone: 720-938-6794
e-mail: *Jackson@littlebigcat.com*
www.littlebigcat.com

Cats International offers free advice for your feline behavior problems and questions.

Cats International
193 Granville Road
Cedarburg, WI 53012
Behavior hotline: 262-375-8852
www.catsinternational.org

Animal Radio

Animal Radio produces educational programming for animal lovers everywhere. Its number one show, *Animal Radio*, airs in more than seventy markets and online at *www.AnimalRadio.com*. Every week, animal experts from all around the world converge to educate pet guardians about responsible pet care.

Animal Radio
233 East 330 North
Kanab, UT 84741
Phone: 435-644-5992
www.AnimalRadio.com

Cat Books

Cat Health and Care

Cat Massage: A Whiskers to Tail Guide to Your Cat's Ultimate Petting Experience, by Maryjean Ballner. New York: Saint Martin's Press, 1997.

Cats Naturally: Natural Rearing for Healthier Domestic Cats, by Juliette de Baïracli-Levy. London, Boston: St. Martin's Press, 1991.

Dr. Pitcairn's Complete Guide to Natural Health for Dogs & Cats, by Richard H. Pitcairn, DVM, PhD, and Susan Hubble Pitcairn. Emmaus, PA: Rodale Books, 1995. An excellent source of pet information.

The Guide to Handraising Kittens, by Susan Easterly. Neptune City, NJ: T.F.H. Publications, Inc., 2001.

The Home Pet Vet Guide for Cats, by Martin I. Green. New York: Ballantine, 1980. First aid for injury/illness.

The Natural Remedy Book for Dogs & Cats, by Diane Stein. Freedom, CA: Crossing Press, 1994. Information about nutrition, naturopathy, vitamins, minerals, herbs, homeopathy, acupuncture/acupressure, flower essences.

The New Natural Cat: A Complete Guide for Finicky Owners, by Anitra Frazier with Norma Eckroate. New York: Dutton, 1990. Also known as "cat queen," Anitra Frazier wrote the bible on cat care. An excellent source for solving cat ailments, information about sick cats at home, and raw food advice, too.

Your Older Cat: A Complete Guide to Nutrition, Natural Health Remedies, and Veterinary Care, by Susan Easterly. New York: Fireside, 2002.

Cat Food Books

Cat Nips!: Feline Cuisine, by Rick and Martha Reynolds. New York: Berkley Books, 1992. Cat food recipes.

Food Pets Die For, Shocking Facts About Pet Food, by Ann N. Martin. Troutdale, OR: NewSage Press, 1997. Describes what goes into pet food. It *is* truly shocking!

Pet Allergies: Remedies for an Epidemic, by Alfred J. Plechner, DVM, and Martin Zucker. Englewood, CA: Very Healthy Enterprises, 1986. The startling facts on why pets die before their time, why they itch or have fleas, and what you can do about it.

Reigning Cats and Dogs: Good Nutrition, Healthy Happy Animals, by Pat McKay. South Pasadena, CA: Oscar Publications, 1992. Raw food diet book.

Super Nutrition for Animals (Birds, Too!), by Nina Anderson, Dr. Howard Peiper, and Alicia McWatters, MS. East Canaan, CT: Safe Goods, 1996. Help for solving problems through nutrition and raw food.

The Cat Lover's Cookbook, by Franki B. Papai. New York: St. Martin's Press, 1993. Cat food recipes.

The Healthy Cat and Dog Cookbook: Natural Recipes Using Nutritious, Economical Foods and Good Advice for Happier, Healthier, and More Beautiful Pets, by Joan Harper, 1992.

Cat Behavior, Tricks, Toys

Cats on the Couch: The Complete Guide for Loving and Caring for Your Cat, by Carole C. Wilbourn. Ivy Books, 1988. Wilbourn is a cat therapist who writes cat behavior articles for *Cat Fancy* magazine.

Do Cats Need Shrinks?: Cat Behavior Explained, by Peter Neville. Chicago: Contemporary Books, 1991. Cat behaviorist.

How to Get Your Cat to Do What You Want, by Warren Eckstein and Fay Eckstein. New York: Villard Books, 1990. Cat behavior book.

How to Toilet-Train Your Cat: 21 Days to a Litter-Free Home, by Paul Kunkel. New York: Workman Publishing, 1991. Has step-by-step procedure on how to train your cat to use a toilet.

On the Road with Your Pet: More Than 4,000 Pet-Friendly Mobil-Rated Lodgings. Mobil Travel Guide, 2004. *www.mobiltravelguide.com*

Show Biz Tricks for Cats: 30 Fun and Easy Tricks You Can Teach Your Cat, by Anne Gordon with Steve Duno. Holbrook, MA: Adams Media, 1996.

The City Cat: How to Live Healthily and Happily with Your Indoor Pet, by Roz Riddle. Fawcett, 1988. Helpful book for cats who are kept indoors only.

The Indoor Cat: How to Understand, Enjoy, and Care for House Cats, by Patricia Curtis. New York: Berkley Publishing Group, 1997.

Train Your Cat, by Terry Jester. New York: Avon Books, 1992. A great book for cat behavior problems.

Twisted Whiskers: Solving Your Cat's Behavior Problems, by Pam Johnson. Freedom, CA: Crossing Press, 1994. Compassionately dealing with cat behavior problems, aggression, new babies in the household.

51 Ways to Entertain Your Housecat While You're Out, by Stephanie Laland. New York: Avon Books, 1994.

Cat Facts

"The Pottenger Cats, A Study on Nutrition," by Francis M. Pottenger, Jr., MD, 1995. Results of a 10-year study showing different effects of raw and cooked diets. *www.price-pottenger.org/Articles/Potts Cats.html*

Cat Facts, by Marcus Schneck and Jill Caravan. Barnes & Noble Books: 1993. Explains cat thought processes, motivations, and behavior. Cat breeds.

Fun Facts About Cats: Inspiring Tales, Amazing Feats, and Helpful Hints, by Richard Torregrossa. Barnes & Noble, Inc., 1998.

Mystic Cats: A Celebration of Cat Magic and Feline Charm, by Roni Jay. New York: HarperCollins, 1995. Cat history, magical beliefs, fascinating folklore.

Natural Cats, by Chris Madsen. New York: Howell Book House, 1997. Cat facts, behavior, and tips.

The Cat Lover's Book of Fascinating Facts: A Felicitous Look at Felines, by Ed Lucaire. New York: Wings Books, 1997. Really fun book of interesting cat facts.

The Life, History, and Magic of the Cat, by Fernand Méry. New York: Madison Square Press, 1968. A most delightful and informative book about cats, and the important role they play in our world.

Understanding Cats: Their History, Nature, and Behavior, by Roger Tabor. Pleasantville, NY: The Reader's Digest, 1997. This book is a good all-around cat fact book. The video is great, too.

Picture Books

CATS, A First Discovery Book, by Gallimard Jeunesse and Pascale de Bourgoing. Scholastic, 1992. A wonderful little picture book for children.

DK Eyewitness Guides: Cat, by Juliet Clutton-Brock. Dorling Kindersley Publishing, 1991. Wonderful picture book for children or adults. A video also is available.

DK Handbooks: Cats, by David Alderton. Dorling Kindersley Publishing, 1992. Beautiful pictures of practically every cat in the world.

Other Resources

People who own cats can get stressed sometimes. I know I do. Managing stress is easier if we have the right tools and know-how.

A Course in Miracles, Mill Valley, CA: Foundation for Inner Peace, 1996.

Nourishing Traditions: The Cookbook That Challenges Politically Correct Nutrition and the Diet Dictocrats, by Sally Fallon. San Diego, CA: ProMotion Publishing, 1995. This is an excellent book about nutrition for people.

Price-Pottenger Nutrition Foundation. This is a nonprofit organization that provides information about food quality for people. It offers books about human diet as well as the Pottenger Cat Study book. Call 1-800-FOODS-4-U or visit *www.price-pottenger.org*.

Local Pet Food Stores and Services

Blue Hills Dog & Cat Shoppe
2255 Main Street, #17
Longmont, CO 80501
Phone: 303-651-2955
Fax: 303-651-2028
www.bluehillsdogandcat.com

Good Samaritan provides a network of foster parents who care for animals until a permanent home can be found. Their mission is to promote healthy relationships between people and their pets.

Good Samaritan Pet Center
P.O. Box 202005
Denver, CO 80220
Phone: 303-333-2291
Fax: 303-377-1625
www.GoodSamaritanPetCenter.org

Friends Interested in Dogs and Open Space
The FIDOS organization of Boulder, Colorado is committed to protecting our natural environment, and ensuring that dogs and their guardians enjoy access to our natural places. Visit *www.fidos.org*.

Computer Consulting
GoodCatsWearBlack.com is maintained with the help of quality Internet services provided by *www.CreativeConsulting.com*. Call 303-415-1000.

Best Blues Musician/Band
Bruce Delaplain, keyboards
blues solo-keyboards, duo, or band available for hire
E-mail: bruce@BruceDelaplain.com

Index

ABCs of behavior, 6
Adopting cats, 17–28
    black male cats, 27
    color/breed/hair length, 26–27
    cost considerations, 25
    health evaluation points, 22–25
    male vs. female, 26
    memories of old cats and, 196
    number to adopt, 21–22
    only cats, 22
    outdoor activity and, 139
    outdoors vs. indoors, 26
    pre-adoption questions, 18–22
    returning after, 27–28. See also New-
        comers
    type of cat(s) to adopt, 19–20
    where not to get cats, 21
    where to find cats, 19, 20–21
Advocacy, 220–27
Aggression, 153–61
    cat fights, 157–60
    causes of, 153–54
    dealing with, 155–57
    declawed cats and, 160–61
    neighborhood cats and, 159–60
    professional help for, 161
    toward humans, 155–57
    what not to do about, 161
Animal Radio, 240
Antifreeze, 12

Behavior. See also Training
    ABCs of, 6
    aggressive. See Aggression
    Annie's view of, 6
    basics of, 8–9
    books, 242–43

cats are like people, 6, 9, 20, 27, 39,
    58, 68, 87, 194
cats showing desires, 137
diet and, 86–88
professional consulting, 239–40
solving problems, 9
squirting with water for, 11, 134
yard deterrents/guards and, 64–66
Black cats, 27, 28
Books, 241–44

Cat beds, 67–69
Cat carriers, 14
Cat fights, 157–60. See also Aggression
Cat toys, 10
Catnip, 96
Changes, 37–45
    going on vacation, 41–45
    moving into new house, 38–39
Chemicals/cleaners, safety, 11–12
Chewers, 189–90
Claws, trimming, 104–6
Collars, 13
Come command, 135–37
Crying cats, 188–89
Curtain climbing, 183

Death, of cat, 195–97
Death, of owner, 15–16
Declawed cats
    aggression issues, 160–61
    exercise/play, 84–85
    grooming (for double-declawed cats),
        109–10
    litter/litter boxes, 54, 163, 173–77,
        207
    massage, 101–2, 103

Declawed cats—*continued*
  safety issues, 14
  walks outside, 141, 151
Declawing cats, 7–8, 35, 201–13,
  222–23
Diarrhea, 124, 125
Diet, 86–99
  Beef Jerky recipe, 91
  behavior and, 86–88
  buying food, 86, 89, 237
  catnip and, 96
  changing, 97
  diarrhea and, 124, 125
  dry food, 87, 92–93
  eating problems and, 96–98
  feeding tips, 94–95, 96–98
  finicky eaters, 88, 97–98
  food books, 241–42
  foods to avoid, 99
  homemade food, 89–92, 93
  for kittens, 94, 97
  for older cats, 98–99
  preservative danger and, 92–93
  quality of food, 87–88
  Quick Dinner recipe, 90
  raw food, 86, 93
  supplements for, 94
  treats, 91–92, 96, 131
  vomit and, 121–22
  water and, 95
  wet (canned) food, 87, 88–89
Dogs, introducing, 40–41
Donation options, 228–30
Dry food, 87, 92–93

Early morning cats, 179–80
Ears, cleaning, 119–20
Euthanizing cats, 195
Exercise/play
  importance of, 73
  kittens and, 85
  lure toys for, 80–82
  older cats and, 84
  with other cats, 80–81, 84–85
  other toys, 83
  outdoor activity, 26, 80
Eye ointments, 118–19

Female vs. male cats, 26
Feral cats, 7, 59–60, 164, 224–27
Finding strays, 59–60
Finicky eaters, 88, 97–98
Fixing cats, 34–36, 226, 227
Food. *See* Diet
Furniture scratching
  protection against, 75–76, 79–80
  reprimands for, 132
  scratching post training and, 75–76

Gender, 26
Gifts, cats as, 25
"Gimme Some" command, 215–16
Grooming. *See* Hair grooming

Hair, losing, 106
Hair grooming
  double-declawed cat support, 109–10
  frequency, 106–7
  shampooing, 109–10
  techniques, 108–10
  tools, 107–8
Hairballs, 26, 122–24, 125
Harnesses, 13, 144
Health
  books, 240–41
  diarrhea and, 124, 125
  food quality and, 86–88
  good, signs, 111–12
  hairballs and, 26, 122–24, 125
  importance of, 7, 111
  of prospective adoptees, 22–25
  signs of illness, 112–13
  vomit and, 121–22
Hitting cats, 129, 134

Holding cats, 100–101, 182–83
Homemade food, 89–92
Housebreaking, 29–30
Household safety tips, 11–13
Houseplants, 10–11

Identification tattoos/microchips, 14–15, 141, 235–36
Illness. *See* Health; Treatments; Veterinarian(s)
Indoor-only cats, 26, 151–52
Introducing new/older cats, 33

"Kiss me" trick, 215–16
Kittens
    with diarrhea, 124, 125
    exercise/play for, 85
    feeding, 94, 97
    handling, 102

Leashes, 13. *See also* Outside walks
Litter box problems, 162–78
    causes of, 163–64
    declawed cats and, 173–77, 207
    identifying multiple-cat culprit, 166
    improving box experience for, 169–71
    last resorts, 177–78
    peeing outside box, 133, 165–69, 238–39
    pooping outside, 124–25
    preventing, 164–65
    suddenly stops using litter, 55
    warnings, 164
Litter boxes, 46–55
    changing/cleaning, 53, 170
    declawed cat considerations, 54, 173–77, 207
    helpful hints, 171–73
    improving experience of, 169–71
    litter sources, 238
    litter types, 46–50

locations for, 51
maintaining, 52–54
pregnancy/birth defects and, 16, 47
safety tips, 12, 16, 47, 48, 164
switching litter brands, 55
toilet training instead of, 55
types of, 50–52
Lost cats
    finding other people's/strays, 59–60
    finding your, 58–59
    microchips and, 14–15, 57, 141
    preventing, 14–15, 56–57
    tattoos and, 14, 56, 141, 235–36
Lure toys, 80–82

Maintenance schedule, 217–19
Male vs. female cats, 26
Massage, 101–3
Microchips, 14–15, 57, 141
Myths about cats, 5

Neighbors
    deterrents/guards and, 64–66
    keeping peace with, 61–66
    their cat/you and, 63–64
    your cat and, 61–63, 142
Neutering, 34–36, 226, 227
Newcomers, 29–33
    first day, 30–31
    first week, 32–33
    housebreaking, 29–30
    into household, 39–41
    introducing to older cats, 33
    kitten special considerations, 31

Older cats
    aging process, 193–94
    diets for, 98–99
    exercise/play and, 84
    final days for, 194–95
    grieving loss of, 196–97
    massaging, 101–2, 103

Older cats—*continued*
  putting to sleep, 195
  replacing, 197. *See also* Adopting cats
Only cats, 22, 102
Outdoor exposure
  benefits of, 138–39
  declawed cats and, 84–85
  exercise/play and, 26, 80
  importance of, 139
  indoor-only cats and, 26, 151–52
Outside walks, 138–51
  benefits of, 138–39
  candidates for, 140
  with declawed cats, 141, 151
  equipment required, 139, 141
  with multiple cats, 150–51
  as privilege, 141
  safety precautions, 140, 149
  timing/frequency of, 140–41
  training phase 1, 143–45
  training phase 2, 145–47
  training phase 3, 147–50
  training preparation steps, 142

Personalities of cats, 17, 20
Petting, 101
Pills, administering, 118
Plants, 10–11
Play. *See* Exercise/play
Pooping, outside of box, 124–25
Pregnancy/birth defects and litter, 16, 47

Raw food, 86, 93
Recipes, 90–91
Reprimands, 131–34
Resources
  advocacy groups, 220–27
  books, 240–45
  declawing information, 208–9,
    222–23
  donation-worthy organizations,
    228–30

feral cat support, 225–27
products and, 231–45
Rewards, 130–31, 135

Safety tips
  cat carriers, 14
  cat toys, 10
  chemicals/cleaners, 11–12
  collars/harnesses/leashes, 13, 144
  declawed cats, 14
  household precautions, 11–13
  houseplants, 10–11
  identification tattoos/microchips,
    14–15, 141, 235–36
  litter boxes, 12, 16, 47, 48, 164
  loss prevention. *See* Lost cats
  outside walks, 140, 149
  pregnancy/birth defects and litter,
    16, 47
Scratches, preventing, 182–83
Scratching posts, 73–80
  basics of, 75
  best times for using, 78
  importance of scratching, 73–74
  training to use, 75–79, 85
  types of, 75, 77
Screen climbing, 183
Scruffing, 134
Shampooing, 109–10
Shopping lists
  adopting cats, 17
  aggression management items, 153
  aging cats, 193
  cat beds, 67
  cat food/supplements, 86
  change management items, 37
  chewer cat items, 180
  curtain/screen climbing cat items, 180
  exercise accessories/toys, 73
  grooming supplies, 104
  litter boxes, etc., 46, 162
  morning-cat issues items, 180

neighbor-relations materials, 61
new cat supplies, 29
outside walk supplies, 139
products/resources for, 231–45
safety/loss prevention items, 10, 56
shy cat items, 180
spay/neuter-support items, 34
training supplies, 129
treatment supplies, 117
urine spraying supplies, 180
vet trip supplies, 111
what not to buy, 236
Shy cats, 186–88
Spaying, 34–36, 226, 227
Spraying (urine), 183–86
Squirting with water, 11, 134
Strays. *See* Feral cats

Tattoos, 14, 56, 141, 235–36
Temperature, taking, 120
Tendonectomy, 205
Toilet training, 55
Touching/holding cats, 100–103,
    182–83
Toys. *See* Exercise/play
Training, 129–37
    basic tips, 133
    biting response, 134
    books, 242–43
    come command, 135–37
    cute cat tricks, 214–16
    general guidelines, 129–30
    hitting and, 129, 134
    for outside walks. *See* Outside walks
    reprimands, 131–34
    rewards and, 130–31, 135
    scruffing and, 134
    squirting water and, 11, 134
Traveling, 41–45
Treatments, 117–20
    cleaning ears, 119–20
    eye ointments, 118–19

pills, 118
taking temperature, 120
tips for administering, 117–18
Treats, 91–92, 96, 131
Tricks, 214–16
    "Gimme Some" command, 215–16
    "Kiss me" trick, 215–16
    "What It Is" trick, 214–15
Trimming claws, 104–6

Urinating outside box, 133, 165–69,
    238–39
Urine
    collecting, 167
    neutralizing, 167–69, 238–39
    spraying, 183–86

Vacation, 41–45
Vaccines, 219
Velvet paws, 181–82
Veterinarian(s)
    cat peeing outside box and, 165–67
    communicating with, 115–16
    euthanizing cats, 195
    finding, 113
    fixing cats and, 34–36
    getting home from, 116
    in office of, 114–16
    trips to, 113–16
Vomit, 121–22

Walking cats. *See* Outside walks
Water, 95
Wet (canned) food, 87, 88–89
"What It Is" trick, 214–15
Wills, cats and, 15–16

Yard deterrents/guards, 64–66

Everything I Need to Know About Cats, I Have Learned From People

by Annie Bruce

Cats and people both enjoy good food and a warm bed,
    Being loved,
    Having fun,
    Getting attention.
We get along with some and not with others.
Our children safe and well-fed.
Our elderly need more help than the young.
    Hating boredom.
    Loving freedom.
First impressions are important.
Routine and habits make us feel secure.
Respect for those who respect us.
Some of us are overweight, some lean, some loving, some mean.
Like to feel superior or good at something.
Like getting new things.
Like to own things.
We'll do almost anything to get what we want.
    A view from a window,
    To sleep in sunlight,
    Fresh air.
We relish and surrender to touch and massage,
Stretching, health, being fit.
We learn from our mothers and fathers.   B.
We learn by watching and doing.   M
Laziness is to be enjoyed.   I
We care for the sick.   L
To smell.   To   C
To touch.   m
To hear.   u   p.
To sense.   j
To taste.   To

To show joy, to have joy, to be joyful, although,
Bad events affect us, too, like moving and changes.
Death of a friend or relative hurts . . . hurts big time.
Separation from our buddies is a real drag.
When disabled we become depressed, frustrated, shy, and prone to
    illness and accidents.
If we get hurt we are more cautious next time.
If we've been hurt it takes longer to earn back our trust.
We will hide when we're afraid and come out when it's safe.
We don't like seeing the doctor, or the dentist.
When we are stressed, we'll show it sooner or later . . . same for when
    we eat badly or don't exercise.
We retreat when we feel inferior or that we don't belong.
We isolate ourselves when we are not feeling well.
Recovery is painful.
We don't enjoy being laughed at.
We challenge newcomers.
We don't consider others important if we're unimportant to them.
If we don't know how to communicate what we want, we snap out, yell or
    feel bad.
But all in all, we manage.
And we do our best to enjoy ourselves no matter what befalls us.
We enjoy recognition.
We feel like hugs sometimes and sometimes not.
We usually welcome company.
We take pride in the things we do well.
Our truest loves, we love unconditionally.
We like to contribute to our families.
We like to try new things and test our limits.
Our eyes show our pain, anger, delight and curiosity.

Oh yeah . . . and most of all?
We love to dance
and sometimes sing.

> Cats are dangerous companions
> for writers because cat watching
> is a near-perfect method of writing
> avoidance.
>
> *Dan Greenburg*

About the Author

ANNIE BRUCE was born in Detroit, Michigan, in 1955, the youngest of six children. Her family owned black cats throughout her childhood. Like her mother and grandmother, Annie has a particular fondness for black cats and has owned black male cats for almost five decades.

Annie attended Cass Technical High School in downtown Detroit and worked for twenty years as a computer operator. Her volunteer work with sick and abused cats took her to public fairs, where she talked to cat owners about their cats' problems. When Annie realized that many owners and cats were suffering unnecessary hardship and expense, she started a consulting business. That business in turn led to this book.

Annie now lives in Boulder, Colorado, with her husband, Bruce, and four gorgeous cats, Marvin-My-Man, Louie-Louie, Mr. Abraham Lincoln, and Bob. When she's not talking about cats, she's enjoying friends, eating, and hip-hop dance classes.

Condensed version of Cat Be Good:
A Foolproof Guide for the Complete Care and Training of Your Cat,
by Annie Bruce, cat owner consultant
www.goodcatswearblack.com

- Diet affects cat behavior. Feed a **wide** variety of food (canned, dry, homemade, leftovers).

- Exercise affects cat behavior. Your cat strengthens his muscles by scratching his scratching post.

- Spending time outdoors improves cat behavior. Unless there are inordinate threats to the cat's safety and welfare, familiarize your cat with the outdoors. Spend time together outside learning the whereabouts of traffic and property boundaries and becoming familiar with passersby. Cats can become "street smart," and this training may save their lives.

- When your cat is bad, simply say "No!" **Don't** say "No" with his name. Use his name only when he is good.

- Do **not** spank your cat or squirt water on him.

- **Always** make it pleasant for your cat to come to you or come home. Say "Hi!" and his name when he enters the room. Reward good behavior with kind words, petting, brushing, hugs, and kisses.

- Adopt spayed or neutered, clawed cats only. Clawed cats need homes and are safer and cheaper to own. **Do not declaw any cat.**

- Play with your cat every day. Use cat toys, not your hands.

PLEASE COPY THIS PAGE AND GIVE IT TO OTHERS.

Important Facts About Declawed Cats

Contrary to what most American cat owners think, declawing does not "save" cats, training time, money, or sofas. It frequently does the exact opposite. Declawed cats can be expensive and dangerous to own because declawing is the number one cause of *litter box problems* and *biting problems*.

- Declawing is an amputation of the cat's toes to the first knuckle of each joint. Declawing removes claw, bone, tendon, and ligament.
- From CourierPostOnline.com, February 1, 2003: "Eighty percent of the cats that are *surrendered* that are declawed are *euthanized* because they have a *behavioral* problem . . . . Declawed cats frequently become *biters* and also stop using *litter boxes* . . . one or the other."—William Lombardi, shelter director, Gloucester County, New Jersey
- A study of 163 cats that underwent onychectomy (declawing), published in the July/August 1994 *Journal of Veterinary Surgery*, showed that 50 percent suffered from immediate postoperative complications such as pain, hemorrhage, and lameness; long-term complications, including prolonged lameness, were found in nearly 20 percent of the 121 cats that were followed up on in the study.
- A study published in the January 2001 issue of the *Journal of the American Veterinary Medical Association* (JAVMA) found that 31 percent of thirty-nine cats that underwent onychectomy or tendonectomy developed at least one behavior change immediately after surgery, with the most common problems being *litter box problems* and *biting*.

PLEASE COPY THIS PAGE AND GIVE IT TO OTHERS.

- A national survey of shelters from the Caddo Parrish Forgotten Felines and Friends indicates that approximately 70 percent of cats turned in to shelters for *behavioral* problems are declawed.

- From the Summer 2002 issue of PETA's *Animal Times*: "A survey by a Delaware animal shelter showed that more than 75 percent of the cats *turned in* for avoiding their *litter boxes* had been declawed."

- According to a study published in the October 2001 issue of JAVMA by Dr. Gary J. Patronek, VMD, PhD, "declawed cats were at an increased risk of *relinquishment*."

- In my own three-year experience, 95 percent of calls about declawed cats related to *litter box problems*, as opposed to only 46 percent of calls about clawed cats—and most of those were older cats with physical ailments. It's been my experience that only declawed cats have cost their owners security deposits, leather sofas, and floorboards. And it's mostly declawed cats that have been prescribed painkillers, antidepressants, tranquilizers, and steroids.

- Declawing is illegal or considered inhumane in many countries, including Germany, Switzerland, Japan, Norway, Austria, Scotland, Wales, and Portugal. On April 7, 2003, the city council in West Hollywood, California, voted to outlaw declawing. Effective May 1, 2003, declawing is illegal in West Hollywood. Similar laws are being considered in San Francisco and Santa Monica, California. See *www.pawproject.com* for more details. Or call toll free, 1-877-PAWPROJECT (1-877-729-7765).

Please copy this page and give it to others.
Thank you,
Annie Bruce
www.goodcatswearblack.com